R

Alvin Pettle
M.D. FRCS(C)

My Prescription for Life

To Sonia
From my
heart to
your heart

Alvin Pettle M.D.
25/05/06

"...becoming a doctor takes education; becoming a healer takes time..."

Library and Archives Canada Cataloguing in Publication

Pettle, Alvin, 1945–
    My prescription for life / Alvin Pettle.

ISBN 0-9736311-0-4

    I. Conduct of life—Quotations, maxims, etc.   I. Title.

PN6081.P48 2004   170'.44   C2004-904601-2

Text Design, Electronic Page Layout & Print Production: Heidy Lawrance Associates

www.drpettle.com

Printed in Canada

To Carol—my beloved wife

*I would never have lived to see this day
without your love and belief in me.*

Alvy
Spring 2004

My Prescription For Life

ALVIN PETTLE, M.D., F.R.C.S. (C)

"I quote others only the better
to express myself,
for others have felt the same as I,
but have said it better."

*I*t was thirty-five years ago, at the end of a very long day, my first day as an intern on call at New Mount Sinai Hospital in Toronto. I was twenty-four years young. There was a short lull at one A.M. and time to take a few minutes of precious rest in the staff on-call room. After the constant, ongoing activity of the day, I felt wound up and couldn't relax. There I sat, restlessly waiting for my next call for help from my fellow human beings.

Luxuriating in the chance to stretch myself even on a spartan cot, I glanced around this dimly lit, sparsely furnished little room. On a shelf was a shabby much-thumbed book that some former occupant had left behind. Almost unconsciously, curiously, I reached for the book. It turned out to be Ebert Hubbard's *Book of Quotations*.

Opening its pages, I began to read. Perhaps because I was feeling a heightened sense of awareness that night, many of the words seemed to enter my very soul and I found myself calmed by their eternal wisdom.

"What comes from the heart, goes to the heart."
THE REBBE

Realizing the positive, healthy effect of this kind of thinking, especially at tense moments, soon thereafter I started a collection of my own, a treasury of thoughts, as I discovered them along the way in my life's journey, words or expressions that I found wise, instructional or inspirational. Each selection had special value and meaning to me personally, and often I would jot down my own reflections or comments below a quotation. Over the years, the collection grew and became a valuable personal resource for my own meditation and spiritual growth and to share with my family, friends and loved ones as that group grew ever larger.

Every day now, I leave one of these thoughts on my answering machine at the office, wanting to share their uplifting, caring power with the people I love, which includes my patients and callers. As often requested, and for at least a decade or more, I have been intending to sort out and commit the whole collection to written form to better share them as a reflection of my life's journey and inspiration.

This became possible when Barbara Davis-Camp, one of my patients, remarked that she was looking for her next challenge in keyboarding, editing and helping to prepare a book, which she regards as her recreational weekend occupation besides being a corporate legal secretary week days. Even my typical scrawling doctor's handwriting didn't discourage Barbara, after 30 years of reading lawyer's handwriting. Using her well-honed organizational and computer skills, she has carefully transformed my collected quotations, thoughts and comments from handwritten journals to these printed words to share with you.

This book is very personal, as I have included some of my original comments below quotations from the time when I originally recorded the thought or reread it as inspiration through my life. When I began, as a hopeful 24 year old, I began to write them down to help build and strengthen my own spirit. Soon, I wanted to share with people I loved and cared for, including my wife, children and now grandchildren, and friends, along the way as life progressed.

These thoughts have profoundly influenced me over the years, comforted me, counseled me, educated me and inspired me. I have always believed they are one of the finest gifts I could share. The odd thing about love is how seldom we actually share how much we care about each other. The beautiful thing about love is that the more you experience it, the more you have to give away. Over the years, I have discovered that I love all the people in my life, not just my family and personal friends, but all my patients and acquaintances as well in the larger ripples of my life pool.

As I have been influenced and inspired, so too I now share these words with you, in the hope that you will also find value in them and choose to pass them on to those you love as well.

To my patients, all of whom are women, please note that in most cases I didn't change the original author's quotes where they used the masculine gender ("he" or "his" or "man") out of respect for the author's creation—many of which were, as you will see, penned and written long before the overdue emancipation of women—but know that I personally think of the word "man" only in the generic sense of "humankind" and cheerfully substitute "she" for "he," "her" for "his" and "woman" for "man" in my personal thoughts and sharing of these wise words.

Also, over the years, some of the author's names were not known or recorded, or have been lost and credit for some quotations was untraceable. An effort has been made to correctly credit all authors wherever possible. Included for your information and interest at the back of this book is a Bibliography of information about the various authors.

Alvin Pettle,
M.D., F.R.C.S. (c)

It has been said that:

If it is the truth, what does it matter who said it? The truth belongs to all of us.

In that spirit, I offer you these, my thoughts. I do hope you enjoy and grow in strength from them. May God Bless each of you. Thank you for sharing your lives and experiences with me.

Take care of each other.

Alvin Pettle, M.D., F.R.C.S. (C)
Toronto, Ontario, Canada
Spring, 2004

ABUNDANCE

Abundance is not limited;
it is the natural state of wealth
surrounding being.

K.G. Mills (1940–?)

ACTION

We learn to do something by doing it;
there is no other way.

John Holt (1923–1985)

Comment: "I've learned that: becoming a doctor takes education; becoming a healer takes time—34 years." A.P.

Words without actions are
a waste of energy.

K.G. Mills (1940–?)

ADDICTION

We are healed of suffering only
by experiencing it to the fullest.

Marcel Proust (1971–1922)

Comment: "Spring, 1994 was when I walked away from allopathic* medicine." A.P.
(*"allopathic"—curing a diseased action by inducing another action of a different kind)

God, give us grace to accept with serenity
the things that cannot be changed,
courage to change the things which should be changed,
and the wisdom to distinguish the one from the other.

Friedrich Wilhelm Nietzsche (1844–1900)

Comment: "Words on the wall before I knew Adam's diagnosis.*" A.P.

(*my son, Adam, was diagnosed with thyroid cancer at the age of 21)

It's easier to repress the first desire
than to satisfy all that follows it.

Comment: "Keep the manhole cover closed. Right Bonnie M." A.P.

ADDICTION

Constant occupation prevents temptation.

There was never a genius
without a tincture of madness.

Artistotle (384–322 B.C.)

Comment: "Listen to your intuition—no matter what the rest of the world says." A.P.

Have the courage to live; anyone can die.

R. Coly

Comment: "Our bodies will perish, our souls, thankfully, never do." A.P.

The public seldom forgives twice.

Sir Wilfred Laurier (1841–1919)

Words are, of course,
the most powerful drug used by mankind.
Rudyard Kipling (1865–1936)

And in the deepest cavern of depravity,
the most sublime souls are held captive.
The Rebbe (1902–1994) Menachem Mendel Schneerson

ADVERSITY

When you are an anvil, hold you still;
when you are a hammer, strike your fill.
John Florio (1553–1626)
Comment: "Carol and I—we have lived this." A.P.

What doesn't kill me makes me stronger.
Friedrich Wilhelm Nietzsche (1844–1900)

In the middle of difficulty lies opportunity.
Albert Einstein (1879–1955)
Comment: "Jerry—I believe in you and I love you." A.P.

The most disastrous times
have produced the greatest minds.
The purest metal comes of the most ardent furnace.
The most brilliant lightning comes
of the darkest clouds.
Artistde Briand (1862–1932)

ADVICE

Every conscious thought,
every utterance of our lips,
every intersection of words with the world
leaves its imprint upon an aura
that surrounds each of us
and stays with us wherever we go.

The Rebbe (1902–1994) Menachem Mendel Schneerson

Comment: "What each of us say and do at all times, matters—the universe holds what we do forever." A.P.

All things have reason;
nothing is impossible.
Every event has its course and purpose.

The Rebbe (1902–1994) Menachem Mendel Schneerson)

AFFIRMATION(S)

Affirmations are like prescriptions
for certain aspects of yourself
you want to change.

Jerry Frankhauser

An affirmation is
a strong positive statement
that something is already so.

Shakti Gawain (1955?–?)

AGING

The more the marble wastes,
the more the statue grows.

Michelangelo (1475–1564)

Be with me, Beauty,
for the fire is dying.

Comment: "Stay with me, Carol*, I do not want to be here without you." A.P.

(*Carol is my wife)

When an old person dies,
a library is lost.

T. Swann (1928–1976)

Comment: "So as we go along through life, we should each write it down, while we can." A.P.

My children's birthdays
make me feel older than my own birthday does.

AMBITION

What do I want to be in life ?
Here I assume a reason for living
that is separate from life.
So many believe that life is
headed towards some grande finale.
But maybe we're not moving in a
direction any more than the earth is.

Hugh Prather (1950?–?)

ANGER

The insanity in holding back my anger
is that I am evidently more willing
to risk destroying <u>me</u> than destroying <u>another</u> person
Hugh Prather (1950?–?)
Comment: Dad, I always loved you, but sometimes I just didn't agree. A.P.

Anger is one of the sinews of the soul;
he that wants it hath a maimed mind.
Thomas Fuller (1608–1661)

It is not the anger of the father but his silence
that the well-born son (or daughter) dreads.
Comment: Lori—sometimes I don't know how I can make the pain go away. A.P.

Anger and hate hinder good counsel.

Fathers, provoke not your children to anger,
lest they be discouraged.
The Epistle of Paul, the Apostle to the Colossians 1:16-17

APPEARANCE

Appearance overpowers even the truth.
Ceos

ASPIRATIONS

Nothing has a stronger influence
psychologically on the environment
and especially on the children
than the <u>unlived</u> life of the parent.

Carl Gustav Jung (1865–1961)

Shoot for the moon.
Even if you miss it,
you will land among the stars.

Les Brown (1912–2001)

Comment: "Jordy—When you step on the stage or off the stage,
you'll always be my star." A.P.

Great God, I ask Thee for no meaner self
than that I may not disappoint myself,
that in my action I may soar as high—
as I can now discern with this clear eye.

Henry David Thoreau (1817–1862)

Ah, but a man's (or <u>woman's</u>) reach
should exceed his (or <u>her</u>) grasp,
or what's a heaven for?

Robert Browning (1812–1889)

NOTE: Underline by A.P.

*In the long run, (women)
men hit only what they aim at.
Therefore… they had better aim
at something high.*

Henry David Thoreau (1817–1862)

*Arguing is a way the ego
has of perpetuating itself.*

K.G. Mills (1940?–?)

Comment: "Mind and ego are just tools—only the soul really matters." A.P

ART

Great art is an instant arrested in eternity.

James G. Huneker (1860–1921)

Art is living stopped in a <u>moment</u> of <u>wonder</u>.

K.G. Mills (1940?–?)

AURA

*Every conscious thought, every utterance of our lips,
every intersection of ours with the world
leaves its imprint on aura that surrounds each of us
and stays with us wherever we go.*

The Rebbe (1902–1994) Menachem Mendel Schneerson

Comment: "Already in this book—maybe saying it twice will
allow this very important advice to stay with us." A.P.

AWAKENED

Only the awakened can waken others.

The Rebbe (1902–1994) Menachem Mendel Schneerson

BABIES

People who say they sleep like a baby
usually don't have one.

Leo J. Burke

Comment: "Thank you, God, for letting me be a part of your work, in being present at 10,000 births." A.P.

BAD TIMES

While a tree with strong roots
can withstand a harsh storm,
it can hardly hope to grow them
once the storm is on the horizon.

The Rebbe (1902–1994) Menachem Mendel Schneerson

Comment: "To my daughter, Trish and my incredible son-in-law, Joel—you two are the next generation—your roots will hold us all for many, many years." A.P.

BEGINNINGS

He who has begun has half done;
Dare to be; begin.

Horace (65–8 B.C.)

Comment: "Write it down now; you have to begin sometime.
Don't let the moment be lost." "Write my Adam—write!" A.P.

BELIEFS

What we ardently wish,
we soon believe.

Edward Young (1683–1765)

BIRTH

Birth is G-d saying you matter!

The Rebbe (1902–1994) Menachem Mendel Schneerson

Comment: "Meagan—you already know this." A.P.

Birth is not an accident.
G-d chooses each of us to fulfill
a specific mission in this world.

The Rebbe (1902–1994) Menachem Mendel Schneerson

BODY

Here in this body are the sacred rivers;
here are the sun and moon,
as well as all the pilgrimage places.
I have not encountered another temple
as blissful as my own body.

Sahara

Comment: "Do not look around outside yourself for peace.
You have peace within you. Be peace." A.P.

BOOKS

Books are the ever burning lamps
of accumulated wisdom.

G. W. Curtis (1824–1892)

BROTHERS

He who understands you
is greater kin to you
than your own brother,
For even your own kindred
may never understand you
nor know your true worth.

Kahlil Gibran, the Prophet (1883–1931)

Comment: "Alex Mostovoy, Shelly Berger, Benji Merzel—you truly do understand."
A.P.

A brother may not be a friend,
but a friend will always be a brother.

He who seeks a faultless brother
will have to remain brotherless.

Comments: —"Let's face the truth, brothers—we all have faults—
but it will never stop us from loving each other." A.P.

"—to my brothers, Shelly and Jerry, with love." A.P.

CANDLES

My candle burns at both ends.
It will not last the night.
But, oh, my foes, and oh, my friends,
It gives a lovely light.

Edna St. Vincent Millay (1892–1950)

Comment: "Goodnight, Neville.*" A.P.
(*Neville was a good friend and surgeon, who died
in his early forties, as the result of injuries sustained
in a car accident when returning from work at 3:00 A.M.)

CHANCE

A chance of a lifetime in a life time of chance.

Dan Fogelberg (1951–?) Partial lyric in "Run for the Roses"

The harder you work, the luckier you get.
Gary Player (1935–?)

Behold the Turtle—
He makes progress only when he sticks his neck out.
James Bryant Conant (1893–1978)

Chance favors the prepared mind.
Louis Pasteur (1822–1895)

CHANGE

Times will change for the better when you change.
Things do not change; we change.
Kahlil Gibran, the Prophet (1883–1931)

The first demand of <u>change</u> is to question belief.
K.G. Mills (1940?–?)

Comment: "Progesterone Cream." A.P.

True life is lived when tiny changes occur.
Count Leo N. Tolstoy (1828–1910)

CHARACTER

Character is destiny.

Hericlitus (5th Century B.C.)

Comment: "Walter, you are a wonderful character—may you fulfill your destiny" A.P.

CHILDHOOD

The childhood shows the man, (or woman)
as morning shows the day.

John Milton (1608–1674)

CHILDREN

The great man is he who
does not lose the child's heart.

Mencius (372–289 B.C.)

Comment: "I love watching Bill* play hockey with Mitch.**" A.P.
(*Bill is my brother-in-law, **Mitch is my grandson.)

He who takes the child by the hand
takes the mother by the heart.

Comment: "Lori*—you were only sixteen—my hand is still there." A.P.
(*Lori is Carol's first daughter.)

Children have more need of models than of critics.

What is learned in the cradle lasts to the grave.

> Comment: "Thank you, Mother; I will never forget you." A.P.

Who goes himself is earnest—
who sends, is indifferent.

> Comment: "Jordy, Adam*—we played together." A.P.
(*Jordy and Adam are my boys from Naomi—thank you Naomi.) A.P.

You can do anything with children
if you only play with them.

Prince Otto von Bismarck (1815–1898)

Comment: "Jory, Meagan, Rachel, Mitchell, Matthew and Andrew*—
I wish I could play with you every day." A.P.
(*These are my much loved grandchildren.)

You may give them your love
but not your thoughts—
For they love their own thoughts.
You may house their bodies
but not their souls.
For their souls dwell
in the land of tomorrow,
which you cannot visit,
not even in your dreams.
You may strive to be like them,
but seek not to make them like you.
For life goes not backward
nor tarries with yesterday—
Be like the archer
who holds the bow steady
and guides the arrow into the air,
and know you can never see where it lands.

Kahlil Gibran, The Prophet (1883–1931)

Comment: "To my children Lori, Sharon, Trish, Jordy and Adam." A.P.

CHOICES

Two roads diverged in a wood,
and I took the one less traveled by,
and that has made all the difference.

Comment: "Follow your heart and make your own path in life." A.P.
"Leboyer, intergrative medicine, etc." A.P.

COMMITMENT

Commitment is never an act of moderation.

K.G. Mills (1940?–?)

COMMUNICATION

If you can solve the knot with the tongue,
do not solve it with the teeth.

I talk because I feel, and I talk to you
because I want you to know how I feel.

Hugh Prather (1950?–?)

Comment: "To Hugh: I have never met you, but I would have liked to." A.P.

COMPASSION

Compassion is the best gift
you can give to others.

Comment: "Jory (Jory is my oldest grandchild)—even at the age of 12—
you already have this wonderful gift." A.P.

What is the difference
between kindness and compassion?
Kindness gives to another.
Compassion knows no "other."

Comment: "Thank you Snezana." A.P.

COMMON SENSE

Common sense is not so common.

François Voltaire (1694–1778)

Comment: "Thank you Fran Garshowitz." A.P.

COMPLAINING

Nothing is easier than fault finding;
no talent, no self denial,
no brains, no character
are required to set up
in the grumbling business.

Small people complain;
big people just do it.

CONFIDENCE

Be sure you're right—then go ahead.

Davy Crockett (1786–1836)

*... if one advances confidently
in the direction of his dreams, and
endeavors to live the life which he has imagined,
he will meet with a success <u>unexpected</u> in common hours.*

Henry David Thoreau (1817–1862)

Comment: "Or her dreams, she has imagined—she will ..." A.P.
(Erin Davis—this is for you)

CONSCIOUSNESS

*Human consciousness is approaching
a great realization—that beneath the veneer
of order and finitude lies a cause beyond mind.*

The Rebbe (1902–1994) Menachem Mendel Schneerson

Comment: "One Universal Soul which we all share—God on Earth." A.P.

CONTENTMENT

*But if a man happens to find himself—
he has a mansion which he can inhabit
all the days of his life.*

James Michener (1907–?)

*He that is content hath enough.
He that complains has too much.*

CONTRADICTION

Contradiction is a lower degree of intelligence.

Kahlil Gibran, the Prophet (1883–1931)

Comment: "How can you disagree with that?" A.P.

COSTS

Nothing is for nothing,
even if the pasha were thy brother.

Ancient Middle Eastern

The cost of a thing is the amount of what I call life
which is required to be exchanged for it,
immediately or in the long run.

Henry David Thoreau (1817–1862)

Comment: "Make sure it's worth it and then do it with all the passion you have." A.P.
"Michael Coren—you have that passion—keep sharing it with others." A.P.

COUPLES

One is a number divided by two.

Rob Nilsson (1963–?)

COURAGE

*Courage is strengthened
when you share it with others.*

*Courage is the price that life extracts
for granting peace.*
Amelia Earhart (1898–1937)

*He that loses wealth loses much,
But he that loses courage loses all.*
Miguel de Cervantes (1547–1616)

*What matters is not the size of the dog in the fight,
but the size of the fight in the dog.*
Coach Bear Bryant
Comment: "My father said this to me before Coach Bryant used it." A.P.

*A great deal of talent is lost in this world
for the want of a little courage.*

*Life shrinks or expands
in proportion to one's courage.*
Anaïs Nin (1903–1977)

With courage you will dare to take risks,
have the strength to be compassionate
and the wisdom to be humble.
Courage is the foundation of integrity.
Keshavan Nair (1960?–?)

CREATIVITY

We must accept that this creative pulse
within us is God's creative pulse itself.
Joseph Chiltren Pearce (1960?–?)

Comment: "I remember a child-birth, complicated with a prolapsed cord—God and the Universe saved that child—not me; I was just his tool and instrument that day. (See my next book, *What Woman Have Taught Me.*)" A.P.

Creativity is harnessing universality
and making it flow through your eyes.
Peter Koestenbaum (1921–?)

Creativity is the very <u>Source</u> and the <u>wonder</u> of your experience.
K.G. Mills (1940?–?)

Creativity never stops and considers.
K.G. Mills (1940?–?)

Comment: "K.G. Mills, I've never met you—but you *are* truly enlightened." A.P.

The creation of something new is not
accomplished by the intellect
but by the play of instinct
acting from inner necessity.
The creative mind plays with the objects it loves.

Carl Gustav Jung (1865–1961)

Comment: "The truth flows from the pen and those that read it, know it." A.P.

CRITICS

Life is too short to waste—
in cryptic peep or cynic bark,
Quarrel or reprimand.
'Twill soon be dark.
Up! Mind thine own aim,
and God speed the mark.

Ralph Waldo Emerson (1803–1882)

CRITICISM

How seldom we weigh our neighbor
in the same balance as ourselves.

Thomas à Kempis (1379–1471)

The cynic is the one who
knows the price of everything
and the value of nothing.

Oscar Wilde (1856–1900)

Ever you remark another's Sin,
Bid your own conscience look within.

CURIOSITY

Satisfaction of one's curiosity
is one of the greatest
sources of happiness in life.
Linus C. Pauling (1901–1994)

DAY

Every day arises to be graced
by your conscious attention to detail.
Each day sets so that you may glean
what you have brought to your place in the sun.
K.G. Mills (1940?–?)
Comment: "Live life moment by moment—right, Eckhart*?" A.P.
(*Eckhart is Eckhart Tolle, author of *The Power of Now,*
a wonderful guide to spiritual enlightenment)

DAWN

It is always darkest
just before the day dawneth.
Thomas Fuller (1608–1661)
Comment: "Jerry, I saw mom crying when Michael died—
two days later you were born and I saw her smile again." A.P.

DEATH

Death is Nature's way of telling you to Slow Down.

Bumper Sticker—Seen in the 1960s

Let us endeavor to live
that when we come to die,
even the undertaker will be sorry.

Mark Twain (1835–1910)

(pen name of Samuel Longhorne Clemens)

To retire is to begin to die.

Pablo Casals (1876–1973)

Comment: "Never retire from life—make moments to remember,
instead of money, when you retire from your work,
take the time to become aware of why we are here." A.P.

Bravery is being the only one who knows you're afraid.

F. P. Jones

Comment: "A reminder of the Aquanamatos.*" A.P.

(*from an often-quoted inspirational speech to nurses given at
their graduation, originally made by Sir William Osler)

The sun is gone down while it was yet day.

Jeremiah 15:9

Comment: "Neil, Neville, Marjorie, Michelin*,—where did you go?" A.P.

(*These are two doctors and two nurses who were my friends
and who all passed away much too young, you are all sadly missed.)

He begins to die who quits his (or her) desires.

G. Herbert (1593–1633)

NOTE: Underline addition by A.P.

Look, I really don't want to wax philosophic,
but I will say that if you're alive,
you got to flop your arms and legs,
and you got to make a lot of noise,
because life is the very opposite of death.

Mel Brooks (1926–?)

Comment: "Actually Mel, birth and death are opposites—life has no opposite." A.P.

Death: No one goes away
and then comes back.

The Song of Harper (2650–2600 B.C.)

Comment: "True for the body—but not the soul;
it continues to live with us always.

—Mom still sits in my office; Dad recently joined her.

—their pain is gone and now they have each other again." A.P.

There is no way to replace
a departed loved one,
for each person is a complete world.

The Rebbe (1902–1994) Menachem Mendel Schneerson

Comment: "And they should be treated that way, with respect—while they are alive,
as well as in memory." A.P.

After all is said and done—
death is still an incomprehensible,
devastating experience
to those who are left behind.
After all the rationalization,
all the explanation,
the heart still cries—and it should.

The Rebbe (1902–1994) Menachem Mendel Schneerson

Comment: "I still weep for those that I loved." A.P.

DEPRESSION

In every Winter's heart
there is a quivering Spring
and behind the vale of each night
there is a smiling dawn.

Thomas Fuller (1608–1661)

In a dark time, the eye begins to see.

Theodore Roethke (1908–1963)

Comment: "Spring 1994." A.P.

Comment: Adam's play—after cancer surgery. "He grew a new pair of eyes." A.P.

Truly, it is in the darkness
that one finds the light,
so when we are in sorrow,
then this light is nearest to all of us.

Meister Eckhart (1260–1328)

DEEDS

*Every good deed ultimately
affects the entire world.*

The Rebbe (1902–1994) Menachem Mendel Schneerson

DESIRE(S)

*Let us train our minds to desire
what the situation demands.*

Lucius Annaeus Seneca (4–65 B.C.)

*The road to the Inn
is always better than the Inn.*

Miguel de Cervantes (1547–1616)

Comment: "Don't rush—this moment never comes again—you're already there." A.P.

*One that desires to excel
should endeavor it
in those things that are
in themselves most excellent.*

Epictetus (55–136 A.D.)

DESTINY

Destiny is not a matter of chance;
it is a matter of choice.
It is not a thing to be waited for;
it is a thing to be achieved.

William Jennings Bryan (1860–1925)

Man is asked to make of himself
what he is supposed to become
to fulfill his destiny.

Paul Johannes Tillich (1886–1965)

Comment: "Replace man with woman." A.P.

Your life is always leading you
toward your destiny,
and every single movement
is meaningful and precious.

The Rebbe (1902–1994) Menachem Mendel Schneerson

DETERMINATION

The secret of success
is the constancy of purpose.

Benjamin Disraeli (1804–1881) 1st Earl of Beaconsfield

Keep a diary, and someday your diary will keep you.

Mae West (1893–1980)

Comment: "Intern day I started this book and will finish with it, only with my last breath." A.P.

DIFFERENCES

*But we are not meant
to all be the same
and differences are as valuable to our Creator
as our similarities.*

The Rebbe (1902–1994) Menachem Mendel Schneerson

Comment: "Remember that before you *judge* a culture or a person with disrespect." A.P.

DIFFICULTY

*It is not because things are difficult
that we do not dare;
it is because we do not dare
that they are difficult.*

Lucius Annaeus Seneca (4 B.C.–65 A.D.)

DIGNITY

*Remember that age is dignity,
that age is wisdom.*

The Rebbe (1902–1994) Menachem Mendel Schneerson

Comment: "To Maggie Burston—thank you for always inspiring me at the office. Maggie is the 80-year-old homeopathic doctor who has spent her life healing others."
A.P.

DIRECTION

I find the great thing in this world
is not so much where we stand
as in what direction we are moving.

Oliver Wendell Holmes (1841–1935)

DISEASE

What cannot be cured must be endured.

Comment: "My neck—my pain—my acceptance." A.P.

DISCOVERY

One doesn't discover new lands
without consenting
to lose sight of the shore
for a long time.

André Cide

Comment: "Or said another way, you can't steal second base
without taking your foot off first." A.P.

A Discovery is said to be
an accident
meeting a prepared mind.

Albert von N. Szent-Gyorgyi (1893–1986)

Comment: "Bio-identical Hormones." A.P.

DISCIPLINE

*Discipline is not
something that is imposed;
it is a way of living
with a clear intention.*

DOCTOR

*Some patients,
though conscious that their condition is perilous,
recover their health simply
through the contentment
with the goodness of the physician.*

Hippocrates (460–377 B.C.)

*Honor a physician with the honors due unto him
for the uses which ye may have of him,
for the Lord hath created him.*

Eccliasties 38:1

Comment: or "her." A.P.

*The art of medicine consists
of amusing the patient
while nature cures the disease.*

Francois M.A. Voltaire (1694–1778)

Comment: "This may offend some doctors… but I don't think
Voltaire's sense of humour should be overlooked." A.P.

To be needed in other human lives;
is there anything greater
or more beautiful in this world?

David Grayson (1870–1946) pen name of Ray Stannard Baker

Comment: "Being allowed to be present at 10,000 births—thank you, G-d."
"Now I sit with grandmothers and we all can reflect." A.P.

DOING

To mean well is nothing
without to do well.

Titus Maccius Plautius (254–184 B.C.)

Things won are done;
joy's soul lies in the doing.

William Shakespeare (1564–1616)

Whatever is worth doing at all
is worth doing well.

Philip Dormer Stanhope, Earl of Chesterfield (1694–1773)

Comment: "Trish—for now, your children are your career and no one does it better."
A.P.

If you want a thing done,
do it yourself.

Jean Jacques Rousseau (1712–1778)

Comment: "Also—if you want a thing done—give it to a busy person." A.P.

You only need to decide to do the right thing
and then God will guide you on your path.

The Rebbe (1902–1994) Menachem Mendel Schneerson

Comment: "I have found—without a doubt—this is so true." A.P.

We will do
and then we will understand.

The Rebbe (1902–1994) Menachem Mendel Schneerson

Comment: "Bio-identical hormone replacement." A.P.

DOUBT

If the sun and moon should doubt,
they'd immediately go out.

William Blake (1757–1827)

Comment: "Never ever doubt yourself—if it feels right,
do it and do it with confidence." A.P.

DREAMS

You see things—you say "Why?"
But I dream things that never were
and say: "Why not?"

George Bernard Shaw (1856–1950)

Comment: "Write, Adam*, write." A.P.

(*Adam is my son who is a playwright; this is also for others who dream that they may create.)

Undoubtedly, we become what we envisage.

Claude M. Bristol (1891–1951)

Comment: "Jordy—Envision it all." (Jordy is my son, the actor.) A.P.

EARLY RISER

I have all my life long been lying 'til noon;
yet I tell all young men,
and I tell them with great sincerity,
that nobody who does not rise early
will ever do any good.

Samuel Johnson (1709–1784)

EDUCATION

He that lives well is learned enough.

Education is life itself; it never ends.

The Rebbe (1902–1994) Menachem Mendel Schneerson

Comment: "I always try and tell all my medical colleagues, that our education *began* at the *end* of medical school and it should never end—thank you patients for reminding me each and every day of my life." A.P.

EGO

In your struggle to be real,
to be centered, to be you,
have you left a place for me ?

Hugh Prather (1950?–?)

Whatever you can do,
or dream you can,
begin it.

W. H. Murray (1913–1986)

The less people speak of their greatness,
the more we think of it.

Francis Bacon (1561–1626)
Baron Verulam of Verulam
Viscount St. Albans

He that falls in love with himself
will have no rivals.

EMOTIONS

There are two worlds:
the world that we can measure with line and rule
and the world we feel with our heart's imagination.

Leigh Hunt

Water in the eyes
is a sign of fire in the heart.

The Rebbe (1902–1994) Menachem Mendel Schneerson

A soft branch breaks not.

The Rebbe (1902–1994) Menachem Mendel Schneerson

ENEMIES

*Just as tall trees are known by their shadows,
so are good men by their enemies.*

Chinese Proverb (300 B.C.)

ENLIGHTENMENT

*As we awaken to who we really are,
we become aware that every detail of life
has meaning and purpose—
every step is a decision—
every move is deliberate.*

ENVY

*Envy, the meanest of vices,
creeps on the ground like a serpent.*

Ovid (43 B.C.–18 A.D.)

Publus Ovidius Naso

ETERNAL

*You cannot have a perspective
on the Ageless or the Eternal
if you are constantly utilizing
the perspective of a mortal.*

K.G. Mills (1940?–?)

EXERCISE

He who fatigues his body—brings peace to his mind.

Plato (428–348 B.C.)

Comment: "My brother, Shelly (the lawyer)—teaches spin classes." A.P.

I will tell you what I have learned myself.
For me, a long five or six mile walk helps.
And one must go alone and every day.

Brenda Welland

EXISTENCE

None of us are here by accident.
We are here because God wanted us to exist.
It is up to us to find out why.

Comment: "Sharon*, you have found peace. Be happy." A.P.

(*Sharon is my daughter; this is to encourage all who seek the "why.")

EXPECTATIONS

What I think I want from someone else
is really what I want from myself.

Hugh Prather (1950?–?)

Expect your every need to be met;
expect the answer to every problem;
expect abundance on every level;
expect to grow spiritually.

Eileen Caddy (1930–?)

Comment: "Lori—expect all this and it will be yours." A.P.

EXPERIENCE

Has any man (or woman) attained an inner harmony
by pondering the experience of others.
Not since the world began.
He (or she) must pass through the fire.

Norman Douglas (1868–1952)

FAILURE

There is no failure except
in no longer trying.

Elbert Hubbard (1856–1915)

Comments: "I read this as an intern in 1969—wrote it down 35 years ago,
and I still find it a useful reminder today." A.P.

Failure is wasted
if you return only to the place
where you fell.

The Rebbe (1902–1994) Menachem Mendel Schneerson

Comment: "Come on Jerry—let's go." A.P.

FAITH

Faith is the force of life.

Count Leo N. Tolstoy (1828–1910)

Without faith a man can do nothing;
with it all things are possible.

Sir William Osler, M.D. (1849–1919)

Comment: "Inspirational doctor—gifted teacher and healer." A.P.

Doubt whom you will,
but never yourself.

Christian Bouee

Reason may tell us how to live,
but faith tells us why we live.

The Rebbe (1902–1994) Menachem Mendel Schneerson

FAMILY–LARGE

Happiness is the one commodity
that multiplies by dividing it.

Comment: "Don and Ann, Herb and Fran,
may we *always* share in the joys of our children." A.P.

FATE

I am the master of my fate.
I am the captain of my soul.

W. E. Henley (1849–1903)

FATHER

The days of your years are threescore years and ten;
and if by reason of strength they be fourscore years,
yet is their strength, labor and sorrow;
for it is soon cut off, and we fly away.

Psalms 90: 10

Comment: "My father passed away when he was 75 years of age;
my mother left us when she was only 59; my solace is that
I know that they have found each other again." A.P.

Why in the hell __am__ I trying to
reform (change) my Father?

Hugh Prather (1950?–?)

Comment: "Hugh (Prather)—hopefully, you and I will meet one day." A.P.

Better is the life of a poor man in a mean cottage
than richest fare in another
man's (__or woman's__) house.

Eccliasticus 28: 22

Comment: "Dad learned this." A.P.
NOTE: Underlines by A.P.

The enemy of thy father, as long as he lives,
will never be thy friend.

Honor thy father
and thy sons shall honor thee.
Oriental Saying

Do not sit down in a place where they
might command thee: "Get up."

> Comment: "When I was a boy, my father told me a story.
> His boss said to him: "Get out of that chair."
> My father told me to be my own boss so that no one
> could ever order me to get out of my chair." A.P.

FEAR

We have nothing to fear but fear itself.
Sir Winston Churchill (1874–1965)

Fear is the static that prevents
me from hearing my intuition.
Hugh Prather (1950?–?)

Comment: "Meditation clears static and opens channels to the Universal Messages."
A.P.

To live a creative life,
we must lose our fear of being wrong.
Joseph Chilton Pearce (1950±–?)

FEELINGS

Man (or woman) take
more pains to mask than mend.
Comment: "Ego and mind mask—but it is the soul that mends." A.P.

FIDELITY

Commitment is never
an act of moderation.
Fidelity is never an act of option.
K.G. Mills (1940?–?)
Comment: "Why try and improve something that is right?" A.P.

FORGIVENESS

To be wronged is nothing
unless you continue to remember it.
Confucius (551–479 B.C.)

The perfection of forgiveness
is not to mention the suffered wrong.

Doing an injury puts you below your enemy;
Revenging one makes you even to him;
Forgiving it sets you above him.

FRIENDS

Your friend is your needs answered.

Kahlil Gibran, the Prophet (1883–1931)

Comments: "Thank you, Alex*, for being there when my Dad was sick." A.P.

(*Alex is a homeopathic doctor and friend who was caring and supportive of my father when he was dying, I will always remember you standing beside me at his bedside.)

A faithful friend is the medicine of life.

Eccliastes: 6:16

Comment: "Thank you Cindi Brand—we love you." A.P.

The only reward of virtue is virtue;
the only way to have a friend is to be one.

Ralph Waldo Emerson (1803–1882)

Be slow in choosing a friend,
and slower in changing.

Comment: "Shelly Berger*—we go back the farthest—let's make it all the way." A.P.

(*Shelly Berger and I share 50 years of friendship.)

Who asks more of a friend than he can bestow
deserves to be refused.

Comment: "I will never again ask a friend for a loan." A.P.

He that ceases to be a friend
never was a good one.

FRIENDSHIP

Real friendship is an unshakeable faith
in what was once truly seen,
no matter how recently or long ago.

Hugh Prather (1950?–?)

FUTURE

The best thing about the future
is that it comes only one day at a time.

Abe Lincoln (1809–1865)

Comment: "Actually, now comes one moment at
a time—the future is tomorrow's moment." A.P.

GAMBLING

Hiding beneath the evil lies
the greatest good,
awaiting your discovery.

The Rebbe (1902–1994) Menachem Mendel Schneerson

GIFTS

Let the season of giving be yours,
not that of your inheritors.

Kahlil Gibran, the Prophet (1883–1931)

Comment: "We have to leave good memories." A.P.
"Money gets spent—I pray the memories will last a lifetime." A.P.

The giver makes the gift precious.

Comment: "Never remind someone that you once gave them
something—a gift is a gift, it is not a debt." A.P.

GIVING

To ask for something back for what is given
is to never have given anything at all.

Alvin Pettle (1945–?)

Wealth is proportional to unselfishness.

K.G. Mills (1940?–?)

GLORY

It's better to be a has-been
than a never-was.

Bear shame and glory
with an equal peace
and an ever tranquil heart.

Hinduism (4000 to 2000 B.C.)

GOD

Yea, though I walk through
the valley of the shadow of death,
I will fear no evil,
for thou art with me,
they rod and thy staff, they comfort me.

Psalm 23

To believe in God is impossible—
not to believe in Him is absurd.

François M.A. Voltaire (1694–1778)

How you treat others is how God treats you.
How you forgive them is how He forgives you.
How you see them is how He sees you.

The Rebbe (1902–1994) Menachem Mendel Schneerson

GOOD

Every good thought you think
is contributing its share
to the ultimate result
of your life.

Grenville Klesser

GOODNESS

Despite our setbacks,
despite our confusion,
despite our pain;
we remain absolutely confident
that goodness will prevail.

The Rebbe (1902–1994) Menachem Mendel Schneerson

Think good
and it will be good.

The Rebbe (1902–1994) Menachem Mendel Schneerson

GOSSIP

He who repeats the ill he hears of another
is the true slanderer.

Comment: "My friends, please don't tell me gossip, it only increases the suffering." A.P.

He who gossips to you
will also gossip about you.

Thou shalt not go up and down
as a talebearer among they people.

Leviticus 19:16

Keep thy tongue from evil,
and thy lips from speaking guile.

Psalms 34:13

Whether it be to friend or foe,
talk not of other men's lives.

Eclesiasticus 19:8

GREED

Thinking to get all at once
all the gold the goose could give,
he killed it and opened it
only to find nothing.

GRIEF

Grief is the agony of an instant;
the indulgence of grief is
the blunder of a lifetime.

Benjamin Disraeli (1804–1881) 1st Earl of Beaconsfield

GROWTH

Every blade of grass has its angel
that looks over it
and whispers, "Grow, grow."

The Talmud (400–600 A.D.)

(Written Judaic Law and Commentaries)

Comment: "What a beautiful image that is." A.P.

We will grow when we remember
we are not what we appear to be.

The Rebbe (1902–1994) Menachem Mendel Schneerson

GUILT

Forgiveness is the willingness to begin.
Guilt is the love of staying stuck.

Hugh Prather (1950?–?)

HAPPINESS

No one can make you unhappy
without your consent.

Happiness is something you cannot pour on others
without getting a few drops on yourself.

Happiness grows at our own firesides
and is not to be picked in strange gardens.

Douglas Jerrold (1803–1857)

Comment: "Yes, travel the world to know humankind—but only when you get home, will you know yourself." A.P.

HATE

To hate and to fear is to be psychologically ill.
It is, in fact, the consuming illness of our time.
H.A. Overstreet (1875–1970)
Comment: "Hate and fear end your life—peace and compassion begin it." A.P.

HARM

None but myself did me any harm.
Napoleon Bonaparte (1769–1821)

HEALING

Healing is a matter of time,
but it is sometimes also a matter of opportunity.
Hippocrates (460–377 B.C.)

Heal your body, your soul and then our world.
The Rebbe (1902–1994) Menachem Mendel Schneerson

HEALTH

To keep the body in good health is a duty ...
otherwise we shall not be able to
keep our mind strong and clear.
Buddha (563–483 B.C.)

HEART

There is a word in every heart
that has a sigh in it
if touched aright!

Words that come from the heart enter the heart.
The Rebbe (1902–1994) Menachem Mendel Schneerson

Things of the heart can never be delayed.
Ethel Kennedy (1895?–1990?)
Comment: "Carol* and I know this." A.P. (*Carol is my wife.)

The heart has its reasons,
which reason does not understand.
Blaise Pascal (1623–1662)

The mind cannot contain God,
but deep within the heart, there is a place that can.

As water mirrors a face, one heart responds to another.
The Rebbe (1902–1994) Menachem Mendel Schneerson

HEIGHTS

The highest and most lofty trees
have the most reason to dread the thunder.
Charles Rollin (1661–1741)

HELPING

Help from without is often
enfeebling in its effects,
but help from within invariably invigorates.

Samuel Smiles (1812–1904)

HOME

Civilization begins at home.

Henry James (1843–1916)

Comment: "Trish and Joel understand this." A.P.

He is the happiest,
be he king or peasant,
who finds peace in his own home.

Johann Wolfgang von Goethe (1749–1832)

On children—
better their laughter than a chamber neat.
Only in their mirth is a home complete.

It is not the quietude of a home
that makes it peaceful;
it is the life within it.

The Rebbe (1902–1994) Menachem Mendel Schneerson

HONESTY

One element of maturity
is the realization
that we don't get away with anything.
Hugh Prather (1950?–?)

The first step to greatness is to be honest.
Samuel Johnson (1709–1784)
Comment: "An honest day is a perfect day." A.P.

The first and last thing that is required of genius
is love of truth.
Johann Wolfgang von Goethe (1749–1832)

No man can create great things
who is not thoroughly sincere
in dealing with himself.
James Russell Lowell (1819–1891)

HOPE

To travel hopefully is better than to arrive.

HUMOR

True humor is fun;
it doesn't put down, kid or mock ...
True humor has beneath it the understanding
that we are all in this together.

Hugh Prather (1950?–?)

Comment: "My seven-year-old granddaughter, Rachel, loves my sense of humour—
and I love nothing more than hearing her laugh." A.P.

HURTING

Getting hurt comes
when I am acting too nice
to risk hurting.

Hugh Prather (1950?–?)

IDEAS

An invasion of armies can be resisted,
but not an idea whose time has come.

Victor Hugo (1802–1885)

Comment: "Progesterone Cream and natural Bio-Identical Hormones." A.P.

Comment: "We should thank Suzanne Somers for putting a face to Bio-Identical
Hormones—how much longer will doctors be able to ignore the truth." A.P.

IDEALS

*Align yourself to an ideal
so that another may see it live!*

K.G. Mills (1940?–?)

IMAGINATION

*Two stonecutters were asked what they were doing.
The first said,
"I'm cutting the stone into blocks."
The second replied,
"I'm on a team that's building a cathedral."*

Old Scottish Story

Imagination is more important than knowledge.

Albert Einstein (1879–1955)

*The world of reality has its limits;
the world of imagination is boundless.*

Jean Jacques Rousseau (1712–1778)

*No amount of skillful invention
can replace the essential element of imagination.*

Edward Hopper (1882–1967)

IMMORTALITY

If you want immortality—make it.

Henry Miller (1891–1980)

IMPROVEMENT

Every day, in every way,
I'm getting better and better.

Emile Couse (1875–1926)

INDIFFERENCE

Nothing in the affairs of man
is worse than indifference.

INSIGHT

During (these) periods of relaxation
after concentrated intellectual activity,
the intuitive mind seems to take over
and can produce the sudden, clarifying insight
which gives so much joy and delight.

Fritjof Capta, Physicist

INSPIRATION

What moves men of genius,
or rather what inspires their work,
is not new ideas,
but their obsession with the idea
that what has already been said
is still not enough.

F.V. Eugene Delacroix (1798–1863)

Comment: "Medicine must move forward—learn about prevention and teach it in medical school." A.P.

An inspired message is breathed;
it is not thought.

K.G. Mills (1940?–?)

Comment: "Take a big breath when pondering this thought." A.P.

INTUITION

What I am actually saying is that
we need to be willing to let our intuition guide us,
and then be willing to follow
that guidance directly and fearlessly.

Shakti Gawain (1955?–?)

Intuition reveals a universe
untapped by intellect.

K.G. Mills (1940?–?)

Thinking is a wall to intuition.

K.G. Mills (1940?–?)

Intuition is the instruction
received from the unseen teacher
when you silence the classroom of thoughts.

K.G. Mills (1940?–?)

Comment: "K.G. Mills sounds truly enlightened.
Thank you for sharing your wisdom with the world." A.P.

JOKES

Blessed are the joymakers.

N. P. Willis (1806–1867)

Comment: "Rachel has a joke book—we write them and make them up together." A.P.

JUDGMENT

Never withhold praise.
Before you speak,
bite the tongue of judgment.

KINDNESS

A forced kindness deserves no thanks.

KNOWLEDGE

Perplexity is the beginning of knowledge.
Kahlil Gibran, the Prophet (1883–1931)
Comment: "I'll have to think about that one." A.P.

If you have knowledge,
let others light their candle at it.
Thomas Fuller (1608–1661)

Wear your learning like a watch,
in a private pocket,
and do not pull it out and strike it
merely to show that you have one.
Philip Dormer Stanhope (1694–1773) Earl of Chesterfield

The challenge is only to ignore the doubts
that come to you from the outside,
and allow that inner knowledge
to shine through and guide you.
The Rebbe (1902–1994) Menachem Mendel Schneerson

We all will arrive at the point where
we will not need to look in books
to know what is right;
it will become part of our very fiber.
Our instincts and actions will be in tune
with our souls and with God.

The Rebbe (1902–1994) Menachem Mendel Schneerson

LAUGHTER

A day is wasted without laughter.

N. Chamfort (1740–1794)

Comment: "Joe Baum could always make me laugh—I miss him." A.P.

Laughter is an inner jogging.

Norman Counsins (1915–1990)

At the height of laughter,
the universe is flung into a
kaleidoscope of new possibilities.

Jean Houston (1941–?)

Comment: "When I hear Carol, Sherry and my girls laughing
in Trisha's* kitchen— all is right in the world." A.P.

(*Carol is my wife, Sherry is her sister, Trisha is one of my daughters.)

LEARNING

Personally, I'm always ready to learn,
although I do not always like being taught.
Sir Winston Churchill (1874–1965)

The things that hurt, instruct.

Learning is movement from moment to moment.
T. Krishnamurti (1895–1985)

Real learning comes about
when the competitive spirit has ceased.
T. Krishnamurti (1895–1985)
Comment: "When my body could no longer compete,
I discovered that you don't have to compete to be complete." A.P.

I learn by going where I love to go.
Theodore Roethke (1908–1963)
Comment: "To Bernie Gryfe—a great dentist and a real friend." A.P.

LETTERS

So is a word better than a gift.
Eclesiasticus 18:16
Comment: "Words last forever—gifts rarely do." A.P.

LIFE

Do not take life too seriously.
You will never get out of it alive.

Elbert Hubbard (1856–1915)

Comment: "Dad once said 'They will never take me alive Alvy'
I just wish Dad that you had stayed longer." A.P.

A long life may not be good enough,
but a good life is long enough.

I believe that imagination
is stronger than knowledge,
That myth is more potent than history,
That dreams are more powerful than facts,
That hope always triumphs over experience,
That laughter is the only cure for grief,
And I believe that love is
stronger than death.

Robert Fulgham (1937–?)

This world that we're livin' in,
it's mighty hard to beat.
You get a thorn with every rose,
But ain't the roses sweet.

Life becomes tragic
to him who has plenty to live on
but little to live for.

Every thing has been
thought of before,
but the problem is
to think of it again.

Johann Wofgang von Goethe (1749–1832)

When I am dead,
I hope it will be said,
His sins were scarlet
But his books were read.

Hilaire Belloc (1870–1953)

Let us love wine and women,
mirth and laughter.
Sermons and soda water
come the day after.

Lord G.G.N. Byron (1788–1824) 6th Baron

The examined life is no picnic.

Only a life lived for others
is a life worth while.

Albert Einstein (1879–1955)

Nothing that is worth knowing can be taught.

Oscar Wilde (1856–1900)

When you were born, you cried and the world rejoiced.
Live your life in such a manner
that when you die, the world cries and you rejoice.
Old North American Indian Saying

In the game of life,
even the 50-yard line seats don't interest me.
I came to play.
Comment: "From a poster Lori* gave to me." A.P.
(*Lori became my daughter when I married Carol.)

He that has achieved success has
lived well, laughed often, loved more.
Bessie Anderson Stanley (1879–1960?)
(See also "Success" in this book)

Life is a single letter in the alphabet.
It can be meaningless,
or it can be part of a great meaning.
Jewish Theological Seminar
Comment: "Zeida Eisler* knew this." A.P.
(*Zeida Eisler was my mother's father.)

No man (or woman) is a failure who is enjoying his (or her) life.
William Feather (1889–1991)

Go confidently in the direction of your dreams!
Live the life you've imagined.
As you simplify your life,
the laws of the universe will be simpler.

Henry David Thoreau (1817–1862)
Comment: "David Garshowitz—thank you for sharing your dream with me." A.P.

Slow down and enjoy life.
It's not only the scenery you miss by going too fast—
you also miss the sense
of where you are going and why.

Eddie Cantor (1910–1964)

Often, people attempt
to live their lives backwards.
They try to have more things,
or more money,
in order to do more of what they want
so that they will be happier.
The way it actually works
is the reverse.
You must just be who you really are,
then do what you need to do,
in order to have what you want.

Margaret Young (Stafford) (1892–1969)

Bad will be the day for every man
when he becomes absolutely contented
with the life that he is living,
with the thoughts that he is thinking,
with the deeds that he is doing,
when there is not forever beating
at the doors of his soul some great desire
to do something larger,
which he knows
that he was meant and made to do
because he is still, in spite of all,
the child of God.

Phillips Brooks (1835–1893)

We are all here to add what we can to,
not to get what we can from—life.

Sir William Osler (1849–1919)

The greatest use for life is
to spend it doing something that outlasts it.

Comment: "Writing allows you to speak with those you will never meet." A.P.

Do all the good you can, — Jody Pettle (Berkel)
By all the means that you can, — Ira Pettle
In all the ways you can, — Marnie Pettle
In all the places you can, — Teddy Pettle
In all the times you can, — Ruthie Pettle
To all the people you can, — Michael Pettle
As long as ever you can. — Richard Pettle

John Wesley (1703–1791)

Comment: "To my *brother's children*—carry your name with the love that came with it." A.P.

Life must be measured by thought and action,
not by time.

Sir John Lubbock (1834–1913)

I live for those who love me,
for those who know me true;
For the heaven that smiles above me,
and awaits my spirit too;
For the cause that lacks assistance,
for the wrong that needs resistance,
For the future in the distance,
and the good that I can do.

George Linnaeus Banks (1821–1881)

The Psalm of Life
Lives of great men, all remind us.
We can make our lives sublime,
And, departing, leave behind us,
Footprints on the sands of time.
Footprints, that perhaps another,
Sailing o'er life's solemn main,
A forlorn and shipwrecked brother,
Seeing, shall take heart again.
Let us, then, be up and doing,
With a heart for any fate;
Still achieving, still pursuing,
Learn to labor and to wait.

Henry Wadsworth Longfellow (1807–1882)

Comment: "This should really be on the cover of this book." A.P.

Be not afraid of going slowly;
be afraid only of standing still.

Chinese Proverb (300–600 B.C.)

The only thing that can die
is the thought that life is limited.

K.G. Mills (1940?–?)

Build your world with precious words.
Fill your days with words
that live and give life.

The Rebbe (1902–1994) Menachem Mendel Schneerson

Comment: "Adam—you share your soul with others through your pen,
I'm very proud of you." A.P.

No matter how accomplished we may be,
no matter how happy or wealthy or talented,
at some point we all find ourselves
seeking a deeper meaning in life.

The Rebbe (1902–1994) Menachem Mendel Schneerson

The very fact that God
has granted you another day
means that you have not yet concluded
your mission in life—
there is still much to achieve
in this world for you.

The Rebbe (1902–1994) Menachem Mendel Schneerson

What is life?
It is even a vapor
that appeareth for a little time,
and then passeth away.

James 4:14

Desire, ask, believe, receive.

Stella Terrill Mann (1913–?)

Comment: "Listen to these words Sharon." A.P.

LIGHT

It is better to light a small candle
than to curse the darkness.

Life is no brief candle to me.
It is a sort of splendid torch
which I have got hold of for the moment,
and I want to make it burn as brightly as possible
before handing it on to future generations.

George Bernard Shaw (1856–1950)

Comment: "Share the gift God gave you with the passion in which it was given." A.P.

You could spend your life in
dwelling on the outrages and scandals
and things that are not right—
or you could take a moment
to search for the light.
In the moment of light,
the night will never have been.

The Rebbe (1902–1994) Menachem Mendel Schneerson

LIMITATIONS

There are no limitations
other than what you think.

K.G. Mills (1940?–?)

Comment: "Allow your soul to reveal the truth to your mind." A.P.

LISTENING

Nature has given to man one tongue, two ears,
that we may hear from others
twice as much as we speak.

Epictitus (55–136 A.D.)

LIVING

Because I could not stop for Death,
He kindly stopped for me.

Emily Dickinson (1830–1886)

Add life to your years
while you add years to your life.

He who has a why to live
can bear almost any loss.

Friedrich Wilhelm Nietzsche (1844–1900)

LOOKING

Look and you will find it—
that which is unsought, will go undetected.

Sophocles (496–406 B.C.)

LOVE

To be needed is to be loved.

Draw a circle around your loved ones,
and hate will have to walk the line
and never touch them.

Hugh Prather (1950?–?)

Comment: "Remember the circle of love picture I took of you 3 girls and your mother on our first holiday—please don't let that ever break." A.P.

Neither a lofty degree of intelligence,
nor imagination, nor both together,
go to the making of genius.
Love, love, love—
that is the soul of genius.

Wolfgang Amaedus Mozart (1756–1791)

When I said "yes" to love,
I said "hello" to life.

Comment: "Thank you, Naomi, for giving life to our Jordy and Adam."
"How could any union that gave life to these two incredible young men *have been anything but right*?" A.P.

Anything less than love is not love.
Love does not exclude; it embraces.

I don't exist to like, but I do exist to love.
Contrary to liking,
love demands nothing in return.
Hugh Prather (1950?–?)

Don't strive for love—be it.
Hugh Prather (1950?–?)

The turmoil of the day
fades in the warm quiet of your arms.
Cec Long

Comment: "Carol's arms." A.P.

He who has never loved,
has never lived.
John Gay (1865–1732)

How many loved your moments of glad grace,
and loved your beauty with love false or true—
But one man loved the pilgrim soul in you,
and loved the sorrows of your changing face.
William Butler Yeats (1865–1939)

Comment: "Helen of Troy would step back, if Carol stepped forward. Helen's face may have launched a thousand ships, but Carol's face launched a thousand dreams."
A.P.

You are the only person, without exception,
to whom I can tell all my heart contains.

Thomas Woodrow Wilson (1856–1924)

Comment: "Carol" A.P.

What greater thing is there for two human souls
than to feel that they are joined in life—
to strengthen each other in all sorrow,
to minister to each other in all pain,
and to be with each other
in silent unspeakable memories.

George Elliot (1819–1880) (pen name of Mary Anne Evans)

Comment: "I thank you Uncle Willy for taking such loving care of my Auntie Molly."
A.P.

Pride makes us do things well,
But it is love that makes us do them to perfection.

Comment: "To Steve Roy (Oz Salon) your talent and passion for your work
keep this world, and my wife, beautiful, thank you." A.P.

Love is the harmonizing
Tower which enables
life to evidence a rhythmic way.

K.G. Mills (1940?–?)

Love is the power that cements and binds,
for it knows nothing separate from itself.

K.G. Mills (1940?–?)

Comment: "Sherry and Bill*—we love being with you." A.P.
(*Sherry and Bill are Carol's sister and Bill is her husband,
who are also our very good friends.)

Food and water are elements of the earth
that maintain our physical bodies,
but love is the language of God,
which sustains our soul.

The Rebbe (1902–1994) Menachem Mendel Schneerson

Selfless love means rising above your own needs.

The Rebbe (1902–1994) Menachem Mendel Schneerson

A man's heart deviseth the way;
but the Lord directeth his steps.

Proverbs 16:9

Thy neck is a tower of ivory.

Song of Solomon 7:4

Comment: "Carol." A.P.

God counts the tears of women.

The Kabala (100 to 1000 B.C.)

Comment: "Any man who abuses a woman—is _not_ a man." A.P.

Love, the magician,
knows this little trick whereby
two people can walk in different directions
yet always remain side by side.

Hugh Prather (1950?–?)

LYING

A lie stands on one leg,
the Truth on two.

Comment: "Natural bio-identical hormones versus synthetic hormones." A.P.

MAN

No man ever quite believes in any other.

H.L. Mencken (1880–1956)

MATERIAL THINGS

He races his jeep up and down his ranch
trying to convince himself that he owns it.
Maybe someday he will notice
the billion year old mountains
are laughing at him.

MATURITY

Maturity begins when
you take from life,
but give more

MEANING

Leading a meaningful life means
being able to pierce the outer material layers
and connect to the energy within—the soul!

We are so busy with our daily lives
and so hungry for instant gratification,
we forget—or never take the time to learn—
why we are here in the first place.

The Rebbe (1902–1994) Menachem Mendel Schneerson

We need spirit more than we need matter;
we need meaning more than we need money.

The Rebbe (1902–1994) Menachem Mendel Schneerson

Always be aware that there is
deep meaning in <u>every single action</u>
and <u>every single thought</u>.

MEDITATION

A quiet mind cureth all.

Robert Burton (1577–1640)

Comment: "Silence speaks (E. Tolle)." A.P.

*True meditation is
the beginning of a productive performance.*

MEMORY

Memory should be the starting point of the present.

Comment: "Don't live there; make new ones." A.P.

*Better by far you should forget and smile,
than you should remember and be sad.*

Christina Rossetti (1830–1894)

Comment: "To my brothers Shelly and Jerry—let us remember what we lost when Mom and Dad died, but let us not be sad—for we once had the best." A.P.

MIND(S)

*The mind is its own place,
and in itself can make Heaven of Hell,
a Hell of Heaven.*

John Milton (1608–1674)

Comment: "Spring 1994." A.P.

*Of all the tyrannies of human kind,
the worst is that which persecutes the mind.*

John Dryden (1631–1700)

Comment: "Actually, it is the mind that persecutes us." A.P.

A mind too active is no mind at all.
Theodore Roethke (1908–1963)

Quiet minds cannot be perplexed or frightened,
but go on in fortune or misfortune
at their own private pace,
like a clock during a thunderstorm.

The mind that allows
for knowledge beyond mind
will contain everything.
The Rebbe (1902–1994) Menachem Mendel Schneerson
Comment: "We all have this within us." A.P.

MIRACLE

A miracle or a marvel
is nothing but
the lessening
of the objective confinement.
K.G. Mills (1940?–?)

MISTAKES

Love truth, but pardon errors.
François Voltaire (1694–1778)

Comment: "Especially your own." A.P.

The sages do not consider
that making no mistakes is a blessing.
They believe, rather,
that the great virtue of man (woman) lies in
his ability to correct his mistakes—
continuously to make a new man (woman) of himself (herself).

Wang Yang-Ming (1472–1579)

You will do foolish things,
but do them with enthusiasm.

Colette (1873–?) pen name of Sidonie Gabrielle Claudine Colette de Jouvenel

Don't let what you've done
be the final measure of who you are.

The Rebbe (1902–1994) Menachem Mendel Schneerson

MISSION

Our mission in life is
not to shake up the world
but to fasten its pegs;
not to climb to the heavens
and holler and roar,
but to walk softly
on the ground,
not to create a storm
but rather a dwelling,
an earthly home
for the essences of God.

The Rebbe (1902–1994) Menachem Mendel Schneerson

Comment: "Thanks, Susan*, for bringing all that to Jerry**." A.P
(*Susan is my brother, Jerry's** wife.)

MIZPAH*

And Mizpah, for he said:
The Lord watch between me and thee
when we are absent one from the other.

Genesis 31:48-49

Comment: "This always reminds me of Karen Garscaden**
and her brother's necklaces—this is for you, Karen" A.P.

(*Mizpah means "a Biblical or rabbinical commandment, **Karen, my patient,
wore a necklace bearing the letters: "MIZ"; her brother's necklace carries
the letters "PAH"—a beautiful pledge of mutual family love and loyalty.)

"Her brother is best friends with Steve Mitz, a childhood friend that I miss." A.P.

MODERATION

Use; do not abuse.

François Voltaire (1694–1778)

Moderation is the pleasure of the wise.

François Voltaire (1694–1778)

MOMENT(S)

What you call a moment is
the fractured gaze of the infinite.

K.G. Mills (1940?–?)

No moment is the same as the moment before,
because every moment is a new creation.
K.G. Mills (1940?–?)

MONEY

He that is of the opinion
money will do everything,
may well be suspected of doing
everything for money.

Marrying (or living with someone) for money
is the hardest way of getting it.

Money will come when
you are doing the right thing.
Mike Phillips

Always leave enough time in your life
to do something that makes you
happy, satisfied, even joyous.
That has more of an effect on economic well-being
than any other single factor.
Paul Hawken (1940±–?)

MORALS

If your morals make you dreary,
depend upon it; they are wrong.

Robert Louis Stevenson (1850–1894)

Comment: "Me after I gamble." A.P.

Live as if everything you do
eventually will be known.

Comment: "...because it will be." A.P.

MOTHERS

The hand that rocks the cradle rules the world.

Comment: "Thanks, Mom." A.P.

"Thanks Naomi, thanks Carol—Mothers are G-ds best creations." A.P.

Our fathers may teach us
what we have to do in life,
but it is our mothers
who teach us who we are.

Comment: "See our Web site www.drpettle.com." A.P.

MOTHERS-IN-LAW

Behind every successful man
stands a proud wife
and a surprised mother-in-law.

Brooks Hags

MUSE

The most potent muse of all
is our own inner child.

Stephen Nachmanovitch (1895–1985)

NEGATIVE PEOPLE

If you're not part of the solution,
you are a part of the problem.

Comment: "Negativity will surely bring negativity." A.P.

NIGHT

Night is the mother of thoughts.

J. Florio (1553–1626)

Comment: "The quiet of the night allows the universe to be heard." A.P.

NOAH

And Noah begat Shem, Ham and Japheth.

Genesis 5:32

Comment: "And when I gave life to Adam Noah and Jordan Mark, I gave life to the future, where I may not dwell." A.P.

"Thank you Shush and Abe Teitel—you've been an inspiration to our boys, your love of theatre entered into their souls." A.P.

NOTHING

What you get for no effort on your part
is usually nothing.

K.G. Mills (1940±–?)

NOW

It's enough that
I am of comfort to someone today;
It's enough that I make a difference now.

Hugh Prather (1945±–?)

Comment: "Each of us can be healers." A.P.

The problem is solved when you accept
that happiness is a present attitude,
not a future condition.

Hugh Prather (1945±–?)

Thinking creates the future;
knowing is the now.

K.G. Mills (1940±–?)

The essence of life is nothing but
the burning purpose of this moment <u>now</u>.

There is no other moment
than the one right now.
There is no space more crucial
than the one in which you stand.

NOW MOMENTS

Today is the beginning of the last of your life.

I heard a voice within the tavern cry,
"Awake, my Little Ones,
and fill the cup,
before Life's Liquid in its cup be dry."
Rubiyat of Omar Khayam (1044–1123)

. . . today well-lived makes every yesterday
a dream of happiness
and every tomorrow a vision of hope.
Sanskrit (2nd century B.C.)

If you take good care of the moment,
the years will take care of themselves.

Do what you can,
with what you have, with where you are.
Theodore Roosevelt (1856–1919)
Comment: "To my brother, Shelly and his love, Alex." A.P.

Today is yesterday's pupil.

Benjamin Franklin (1706–1790)

May you live all the days of your life.

Jonathan Swift (1667–1745)

There comes a moment to everyone,
when beauty stands
staring into the soul with sad, sweet eyes
that sicken at the sound of words,
and God help those who pass the moment by.

Edmond Rostand (1868–1918)

Comment: "The birth of every child." A.P.

And if not now—when ?

Hillel (70 B.C.–10 A.D.?)

Write it on your heart
that every day is the last day in the year.
No man has learned anything rightly
until he knows that every day is doomsday.
Today is a King in disguise.
Today always looks mean to the thoughtless, in the
face of a uniform experience that all good and great
and happy actions are add up precisely of these blank todays.
Let us not be so deceived;
let us unmask the King as he passes.
He only is rich who owns the day,
and no one owns the day who allows it
to be invaded with worry, fret and anxiety.

Finish every day and be done with it.
You have done what you could.
Some blunders and absurdities no doubt crept in;
forget them as soon as you can.
Tomorrow is a new day; begin it well and serenely,
with too high a spirit to be encumbered
with your old nonsense.
This day is all that is good and fair.
It is too dear, with its hopes and invitations,
to waste a moment on the yesterdays.

Ralph Waldo Emerson (1803–1882)

Comment: "Please listen Lori." A.P.

Oneself

We will discover the nature of
our particular genius
when we stop trying to conform
to our own or to other people's models,
learn to be ourselves,
and allow our natural channels to open.

Shakti Gawain (1955±–?)

Comment: "My wonderful patients bring this to the office every day." A.P.

Opinion

Something within me
will not let me rest
with the bad opinion of another person.

Hugh Prather (1945±–?)

OPPORTUNITY

Chance favors the prepared mind.

Don't wait for your ship to come in;
Row out and meet it.

Genuine beginnings
begin within us,
even when they are brought to our attention
by external opportunities.
William Bridges (1950±–?)

PASSIONS

Man's passions make him live;
his wisdom merely make s him last.
N. Chamfort (1740–1794)

PATIENCE

Patience may be bitter
but its fruit is sweet.

PEACE

Of one thing I am certain—
the body is not the measure of healing;
peace is the measure.

George Melton (1960±–?)

To me, the sound and the feel
of a baby laying sleeping on your chest is
probably the most peaceful and pleasurable
experience that life has to offer.

Alvin Pettle (1945–?)

Comment: "Jordy*, I still remember you lying on my chest sleeping." A.P.

(Jordy is my first son.)

Only when you've found peace
within yourself
can you help find peace
for the entire world.

For the human being,
inner peace is only achieved
by first surrendering
to the unknown.

Comment: "Surrender is acceptance." A.P.

"I agree with Eckhart Tolle, the author of *The Power of Now*." A.P.

PEOPLE

All the people on this planet
make up a single, magnificent body
with a single soul—
called human kind.

Comment: "That soul is a piece of G-d." A.P.

Something within me knows
that most of what I am
will die without people.

Hugh Prather (1945±–?)

Comment: "I thank G-d each day for allowing me to be a doctor." A.P.

PERSONALITIES

The meeting of two personalities
is like the contact
of two chemical substances;
if there is any reaction,
both are transformed.

Carl G. Jung (1885–1961)

PERSONALITY

A man's character is the
arbiter of his fortune.

Latin Proverb (600 B.C.–1600 A.D.)

Comment: "Benji Merzel, this is for you." A.P.

There are two ways of spreading light:
to be the candle
or the mirror that reflects it.

Edith Whorton

He (she) who under values himself (herself)
is justly undervalued by others.

Wilton Hazlett (1778–1830)

If a man doesn't keep pace
with his companions,
perhaps it is because he hears a
different drummer.
Let him step to the music he hears,
however measured or far away.

Henry David Thoreau (1817–1862)

Comment: "Walter—never lose that light in your eyes, you are special." A.P.

Personality is to a man
what perfume is to a flower.

C. Schweck

Observe the face of the wife
to know the husband's character.

It isn't what I do—but how I do it.
It isn't what I say—but how I say it.

Mae West (1893–1980)

People are lonely because
they build walls, instead of bridges.

> Comment: "One of my patients wrote a book
> called *Take the Step and the Bridge Will Appear*." A.P.

I think, somehow, that we learn
who we really are
and then live with that decision.

Eleanor Roosevelt (1884–1962)

Comment: "Michael M—may your way find you peace." A.P.

Think like a man (<u>or woman</u>) of action,
act like a man (<u>or woman</u>) of thought.

Henri Bergson (1859–1941)

Note: Underlines by A.P.

PERSEVERANCE

Great works are performed
not by strength—but by perseverance.

Samuel Johnson (1709–1784)

Philosophy

This is what you should do:
love the earth and sun and the animals;
despise riches; give alms to everyone that asks;
stand up for the stupid and crazy;
devote your income and labor to others;
hate tyrants; argue not concerning God;
have patience and indulgence toward the people;
take off your hat to nothing known or unknown
or to any man or number of men;
re-examine all you have been told
at school, or church or in any book;
dismiss what insults your own soul,
and your very flesh shall be a great poem.

Walter Whitman (1819–1892)

Play

What we play is life.

Louis Armstrong (1901–1971)

Comment: "Play on Jordy*; Play on Adam.*" A.P.
(My son Jordy* is an actor; my son **Adam is a playwright.)

POSSIBILITIES

As soon as you free yourself
from the walls of belief,
there lies before you
the unlimited vista of infinite possibilities.

K.G. Mills (1940±–?)

POWER

Think of yourself as an incandescent power,
illuminated and perhaps forever
touched by God and his messengers.

Brenda Welland

Comment: "Today I met Victor, a man who heals with his powerful hands." A.P.

PRACTICE

I shall become a master in this art
only after a great deal of practice.

Erich Fromm (1900–1980)

Comment: "This is for you my friend Alex—stay inspired." A.P.

PRAISE

If you think that praise is due him,
now is the time to say it to him,
for he cannot read his tombstone
when he's dead.

Berton Braycett

PREPARATION

Forewarned, forearmed—
to be prepared is half the victory.

Miguel de Cervantes (1547–1616)

PRESENCE

You cannot be half convinced
about being <u>totally</u> present.

K.G. Mills (1940±–?)

PRESSURE

A diamond is a chunk of coal
that made good under pressure.

That which does not kill me makes me stronger.
Friedrich Willhelm Nietzche (1844–1900)

PROMISES

To refuse in a kind manner
is better than to make a long list
of promises you cannot keep.
William O'Brien (1852–1928)

Comment: "I'm still trying to learn this." A.P.

PROGESTRONE

It is liberating,
this trick we have
to discover what works
before understanding how.
The Rebbe (1902–1994) Menachem Mendel Schneerson)

QUITTING

Don't quit when the tide is lowest,
For it's just about to turn;
Don't quit over doubts, questions,
For there's something you may learn.
Don't quit when the night is darkest.
For it's just a while to dawn;
Don't quit when you've seen the farthest,
For the race is almost won.
Don't quit when the hill is steepest,
For your goal is almost nigh;
Don't quit, for you're not a failure
Until you fail to try.

Jill Wolfe

Our greatest glory is not in never failing,
but in rising every time we fall.

Oliver Goldsmith (1728–1774)

QUOTES

I quote others only the better to express myself,
for others have felt the same as I have,
but have said it better.

When you are old, gray and full of sleep,
And nodding by the fire—
dream of the soft look your eyes had once,
and of their shadows deep.

William Butler Yeats (1865–1939)

READING

Reading is to the mind
what exercise is to the body.

Joseph Addison (1672–1719)

Comment: "Carol does both of these to perfection." A.P.

REALITY

The test of Reality:
That which is <u>Real</u> never changes.

K G. Mills (1940±–?)

REASON

The simplicity of the magnificent
is usually lost
because of the complexity of reason.

K.G. Mills (1940±–?)

RECOVERY

Make your own recovery the first priority in yourself.
Robin Norwood (1960±–?)

REFLECTION

*Pause for a moment to reflect
on the true priorities in your life.*

RELATIVES–ANCESTORS

*Then there are our roots,
deep under the ground,
unmoving and serene.
They are our ancient
mothers and fathers,
who lie within us
at our very core.*

Comment:
"To my Zeides* and Bubbes** who sleep with God—your dreams are still alive." A.P.
(*Zeida = grandfather; **Bubbi = grandmother)

REPUTATION

An ill wound but not an ill Name
may be healed.

The reputation of a 1000 years
may be determined by the conduct of one hour.

RESPECT

Surround yourself with people
who respect and treat you well.

Claudia Black (1960±–?)

Comment: "Children remember when they are treated well—I still can remember when my uncle Sy and auntie Carol took me <u>and only me</u> out for my 10th birthday." A.P.

RESPONSIBILITY

The price of greatness is responsibility.

Sir Winston Churchill (1864–1965)

REST

Rest in <u>awareness</u>, not in oblivion.
K.G. Mills (1940±–?)

Rest is not quitting
The busy career;
Rest is the filling
Of self to its <u>sphere</u>.
It's the brook's <u>motion</u>,
Clear without strife,
Fleeing to ocean,
After its life.
It's loving and serving,
the Highest and Best,
The onwards!—unswerving,
And that is true rest.

John Sullivan Dwight (1813–1893)

RESULTS

Demand results from yourself,
not from someone else.

RETIREMENT

No one should retire from life at any age.

REWARDS

The highest reward for man's toil
is not what he gets for it
but what he becomes by it.

John Ruskin (1819–1900)

RISK

That which is necessary is never a risk.

Comment: "My walking away—April 1994*." A.P.

(*at this date, I had to make a major change in my life direction, away from allopathic towards holistic medicine; it was necessary for me.)

The universe will reward you
for taking risks on its behalf.

Shakti Gawain (1955±–?)

Comment: "Medical School and Naturopathic College should share classes, patients need you to *respect* each other." A.P.

ROLE-PLAYING

*How do you know what it is to be a Prince
unless you enact the part.*

K.G. Mills (1940±–?)

ROOTS

*If you see a tree that has <u>endured</u>,
you know its <u>roots</u> run <u>deep</u>.*

K.G. Mills (1940±–?)

RUT

*The only difference between a rut and a grave
is the size of it.*

K.G. Mills (1940+–?)

SECRETS

*Three may keep a secret—
if two of them are dead.*

SELF

*Since you are like no other being ever created
since the beginning of time,
you are incomparable.*
Brenda Welland
Comment: "To my children—and their children—and to all children." A.P.

*Trust in yourself.
Your perceptions are often far more accurate
than you are willing to believe.*
Claudia Black (1960±–?)

*He who knows others is wise;
he who knows himself is enlightened.*
Lao Tzu (604 B.C)

*Public opinion is a weak tyrant
compared with our own private opinion.
What a man thinks of himself, that
is which determines, or rather indicates, his fate.*
Henry David Thoreau (1817–1862)

*Whatever you are by nature,
never desert your line of talent.
Be what nature intended for you,
and you will succeed.*
Sydney Smith (1771–1845)

There is a kind of greatness
which does not depend upon fortune;
it is a certain manner that distinguishes us,
and which seems to destine us for great things;
it is the value we insensibly set upon ourselves;
it is by this quality that we gain the defense
of other men, and it is this which
commonly raises us more above them
than birth, rank, or even merit itself.

Francois due la Rochefoucauld (1613–1680)

SELF–CARE

Saying "NO" <u>can</u> be the ultimate self-care.

Claudia Black (1960±–?)

Comment: "It's taken me a long time to learn this." A.P.

SELF–CONSCIOUSNESS

Inspiration may be a form of super-consciousness
or perhaps of sub-consciousness—
I wouldn't know.
But I am sure it is the antithesis of self-consciousness.

Aaron Copeland (1900–1990)

SELF–DESTRUCTIVENESS

Remember, every thought pattern being held that is not in agreement with your ideals is destructive.

K.G. Mills (1940±–?)

SELF–IMAGE

Keep your self image "<u>clean</u>" and bright. It is the window through which you see the world.

SELFISHNESS

Selfishness is the greatest curse of the human race.

William Gladstone (1809–1898)

SELF WORTH

He who undervalues himself is justly undervalued by others.

William Hazlett (1778–1830)

SEPARATION

*There exists no cure for a heart wounded
with the sword of separation.*

Hitopadesa (5th century A.D.)

SEX

*The two sexes
mutually corrupt and improve each other.*

Mary Wolston Berath

SHAME

*Bear shame and glory
with an equal peace and
an ever tranquil heart.*

Hinelus

SHARING

Remember, whatever you have learned,
whatever you have been touched by,
you must share it with others.

The Rebbe (1902–1994) Menachem Mendel Schneerson

Comment: "Thank you Barbara Davis, for helping me share this book with the
world." Barbara Davis organized these thoughts and typed them for you."
The bibliography was all her own work." A.P.

SILENCE

Silence can also mean confidence.
Silence can mean: live and let live.

Hugh Prather (1945±–?)

No trumpets sound when the important decisions
of our life are made.
Destiny is made known silently.

Agenes de Mille (1909–1993)

SILENCER

If a negative thought should arise in your mind,
be still until you have chased it away.
Do not allow it to pass your lips.

The Rebbe (1902–1994) Menachem Mendel Schneerson

SIMPLICITY

Simplicity is the keynote of greatness—
yet often disregarded
for it is so unexpected as the garment of genius.
What an armor to the man—greatness.

K.G. Mills (1940±–?)

SIN

He that is without sin among you,
let him cast a stone at her.

John 8:7

Hate the sin and love the sinner.

Mahatma Gandhi (1869–1948)

There is not a just man upon earth,
that doeth good, and sinneth not.

Ecclesiastes 7:20

SISTER

As is the mother, so is the daughter.

Jeremiah 16:44

Comment: "Lori, Sharon and Trish—remember the circle of love." A.P.

SLEEP

Sleep, that knits up the ravell'd sleeves of care.
William Shakespeare (1564–1616)

When one begins to turn in bed,
it's time to turn out.
Wellington (1769–1852)

A good conscience is a restful pillow.

SMILE

A smile is the beginning of wisdom.
Comment: "To my patients—may you be smiling often in *your* life." A.P.

SOURCE

Are you kept so busy that you forget the <u>Source</u> ?
K.G. Mills (1940±–?)

Soul

To know what you prefer
instead of humbly saying "Amen"
to what the world tells you that you ought to prefer,
is to have kept your soul alive.

Robert Louis Stevenson (1850–94)

Every time you don't follow your inner guidance,
you feel a loss of energy, loss of power,
a sense of spiritual deadness.

Shakti Gawain (1955±–?)

Learn to get in touch
with the silence within yourself
and know that
everything in this life has a purpose.

Elizabeth Kubbler-Ross (1950±–?)

Comment: "Meditate. Meditation is like watching the movement of your own stars."

A.P.

Every soul that touches yours—
Be it the slightest contact —
Gets there from some good;
Some little grace;
One kindly thought;
One aspiration yet unfelt;
One bit of courage.
For the darkening sky;
One gleam of faith.
To brave the thickening ills of life;
One glimpse of brighter skies—
To make his (or her) life worthwhile.
And Heaven a surer heritage.

George Eliot (1819–1880)

Note: Underlined by A.P.

Comment: "My daily hope with each patient." A.P.

You are not a lackey with a Soul
but a Soul that promises freedom from limits.

K.G. Mills (1940±–?)

Upon every person's soul
there are words written and words engraved.
This and only this is the truth.

The Rebbe (1902–1994) Menachem Mendel Schneerson

In every person there lies all the souls
that ever were and all there ever will be.

The Rebbe (1902–1994) Menachem Mendel Schneerson

*Men and women can never be happy if they do not
nourish their souls as they do their bodies.*

The Rebbe (1902–1994) Menachem Mendel Schneerson

*Without experiencing the soul,
there can be no personal growth.*

The Rebbe (1902–1994) Menachem Mendel Schneerson

*We all have wings—our soul—
that can lift us as high as we need to go—
all we have to do is learn how to use them.*

The Rebbe (1902–1994) Menachem Mendel Schneerson

*We are all caught in this world—
like a fish in a net—
but a net has holes in it—
find one and you shall escape.*

Comment: "… to the eternal truth." A.P.

*No matter how overwhelming
your fears may seem,
give your soul time
to speak to you.*

The Rebbe (1902–1994) Menachem Mendel Schneerson

*Remember that in the journey of life,
your body is the vehicle,
but your soul is the compass.*

The Rebbe (1902–1994) Menachem Mendel Schneerson

We have a brain to process information,
emotions that move us,
but it is our soul that should guide us.

SPACE

The art of an object: to define <u>space</u>.

SPEECH

Such is the mirror of the soul,
as a man speaks, so is he.

Publilius Syrus (1st century B.C.)
Comment: "It is not what we say—but *how* we say it." A.P.

SPEAKING

Silence at the right time is eloquence.

When you speak well of others,
your character speaks for itself.

SPIRIT

If you do not nourish your own
emotional and spiritual needs,
no amount of material success will satisfy you.

The Rebbe (1902–1994) Menachem Mendel Schneerson

SPIRITUAL

"And there is a spiritual way of seeing
which comes to me suddenly—
These times have inspired me to broader visions."

Hugh Prather (1945±–?)

SPOTS

Can the Ethiopian change his skin,
or the leopard his spots ?

Jeremiah 15: 23

Comment: "A surgeon's comment to me, as an intern—1969." A.P.

STRENGTH

The great tests of life reveal character.
It is not until winter comes
that we know the pine is an evergreen.

Comment: "True friends are there at your worst times in life." A.P.
"Thanks Michael M., thanks Bonnie M." A.P.

STRUGGLE

Struggle is an opportunity
to reach the ultimate—
when darkness itself becomes light.

The Rebbe (1902–1994) Menachem Mendel Schneerson

SUCCESS

Speak little of your successes...
less of your failures.

Success is a belief come true.

I cannot give you the formula for success,
but I can give you the formula for failure—
which is—"Try to please everybody."

Herbert George (1593–1633)

If a man can <u>write</u> a better <u>book</u>,
<u>preach</u> a better <u>sermon</u>,
or <u>make</u> a better <u>mouse-trap</u>
than his neighbor,
though he build his house in the woods,
the world will make a beaten path to his door.

SUCCESS

Success means one goal at a time—
MY GOAL NOW—age 59—
is to share this book with you—

Alvin Pettle (1945–?)

Comment: "My next book—*What Women Have Taught Me*—
my goal before I am 65 (G-d willing)." A.P.

The rung of a ladder was
never meant to rest upon;
but only to hold a man's foot
long enough to enable him to
put the other some-what higher.

Thomas H. Huxley (1825–95)

Comment: "Or her foot." A.P.

The most important single ingredient
in the formula of success
is the knack of getting along with people.

Theodore Roosevelt (1858–1919)

Comment: "My father would have agreed." A.P.

That man is a success who has lived well,
laughed often and loved much;
who has gained the respect of intelligent men
and the love of children;
who has filled his niche
and accomplished his task;
who leaves the world better than he found it;
whether by an improved poppy,
a perfect poem or a rescued soul;
who never lacked appreciation of earth's beauty
or failed to express it;
who looked for the best in others
and gave the best he had.

Bessie Anderson Stanley (1879–19--)
Winning entry in a 1904 contest by *Brown Book Magazine*
(frequently miscredited to Ralph Waldo Emerson)
(reprinted by Ann Landers, March 1995)

Behind every successful man
stands a proud wife
and a surprised mother-in-law.

Brooks Hags

The talent of success is
nothing more than
doing what you can do, well;
and doing well whatever you do,
without a single thought of fame.

Henry Woodsworth Longfellow (1807–1882)

No bird soars too high
if he soars with his own wings.

William Blake (1757–1827)

Comment: "I applaud all people who have made their own success." A.P.

I have learned that success
is to be measured
not as much by the position
that one has reached in life
as by the obstacles which he has overcome
while trying to succeed.

Brooker T. Washington (1856–1915)

There is no greater elevation than
having made it on your own.

The Rebbe (1902–1994) Menachem Mendel Schneerson

SUFFERING

Behold, I have refined thee,
but not with silver;
I have chosen thee in the furnace of affliction.

Isiah 48:10

Like the precious few drops of oil
that can be extracted only when olives are crushed,
suffering can lead us to reconsider
the meaning of our existence
and to commit more fully to
our spiritual development.

The Rebbe (1902–1994) Menachem Mendel Schneerson

SURVIVAL

When you can't change
the direction of the wind—
adjust your sails.

SYD K.*

It is better to go to the house of mourning,
than to the house of feasting.

Ecclestiastes 7:2

Comment: "I'll never miss a Shiva** again." A.P.

(*Syd K. was a family friend; I missed attending Shiva for him because I thought I was too busy, but I regret that to this day.) (**Shiva = formal Jewish observance of condolences at death, including emotional support of bereaved relatives after passing.)

SYNCHRONICITY

These things people call
amazing coincidences:
synchronicity, small miracles—
this is the way the world is supposed to work.

The Rebbe (1902–1994) Menachem Mendel Schneerson

Comment: "If we pay attention, our path will be known to us." A.P.

TAKING

In the circle of life,
never take more than you give.

"The Lion King" (1994) Musical Play, first opened New York; also a Disney Movie

TALENT

Use what talents you possess;
the woods would be very silent
if no birds sang there except those that sang best.

Henry Van Dyke (1852–1933)

TALKING

The music that can deeper reach,
and cure all ill,
is cordial speech.

Ralph Waldo Emerson (1803–1882)

Comment: "My mother taught me this." A.P.

Speech is the index of the mind.

Seneca (4 B.C.–65 A.D.)

TASKS

Do not be so willful;
just relax and know within your heart
what you wish to do and see
if the way is not opened for you.

K.G. Mills (1940±–?)

TEACHERS

Teachers affect eternity;
they can never tell where their influence stops.

Henry Adams (1838–1918)

Comment: "High school—Mrs. Heard, Mr. York—thank you for believing in me."
A.P.

Encouragement from a good teacher
can turn a student's life around.

Comment: (See above) A.P.

TEARS

God counts the tears of women.

The Kabala (100 to 1000 B.C.)

Comment: "Any man who causes a woman to cry —is *not* a man." A.P.

THINKING

What you think in <u>private</u>
is your action in <u>public</u>.

K.G. Mills (1940±–?)

THOUGHTS

Great men are they who see that the spiritual
is stronger than any material force,
that thoughts and <u>words</u> rule the world.

Ralph Waldo Emerson (1803–1882)

In every thought,
look for the power to change the world.

The Rebbe (1902–1994) Menachem Mendel Schneerson

TIME

Negative feeling is the thief of time.

Comment: "To my daughter who is in pain—time heals." A.P.

Follow your desire as long as you live;
do not lessen the time of following your desire,
for the wasting of time is
an abomination of the spirit.

Ptallotpe (2350 B.C.)

To every thing there is a season,
and a time to every purpose under heaven,
"A time to be born and a time to die ..."
Ecclesiastes 3:1-8

There is nothing so powerful as truth—
and often nothing so strange.
Dave Webster

Lost time is like a run in a stocking.
It always gets worse.
Anne Morrow Lindbergh (1906–2001)

Better be an hour too early
than a minute too late.
Comment: "Running to Zeida Eisler's unveiling—never again." A.P.

We do well to manage the next ten minutes.
Edward (Ted) M. Kennedy (1932–?)
Comment: "Even that can be broken down to just *this moment—now.*" A.P.

Ordinary people merely think
how they shall spend their time;
a man of talent tries to use it.
Arthur Schopenhauer (1788–1860)

A <u>man</u> for all seasons
is the one who knows he is not
in a time sequence.
K.G. Mills (1940±–?)
Comment: "man and he as in mankind; also, of course woman and she."

In the very point of time, all of time is there.
The Rebbe (1902–1994) Menachem Mendel Schneerson
Comment: "We are the centre of a figure eight—all that has ever been
or that will ever be, passes through each of us." A.P.

Remember that one minute of your life
has all the properties of your entire life.
The Rebbe (1902–1994) Menachem Mendel Schneerson

Each breath, each tick,
each beat of the heart
comes only once.
The Rebbe (1902–1994) Menachem Mendel Schneerson

Nourish your soul
by setting aside a special time each day
to study, to meditate and to pray.
The Rebbe (1902–1994) Menachem Mendel Schneerson
Comment: "Zeida Eisler* knew this." A.P.
(*Zeida Eisler was my mother's father, my grandfather.)

Remember that every moment and every event,
from the most sublime to the most mundane,
is permeated with meaning and purpose
—you just have to remain aware of it.

The Rebbe (1902–1994) Menachem Mendel Schneerson

T.M.*

Meditation is a precious time for
plotting the movement of our own stars.

Comment: "One of my favorites."
(*T.M.–Transcendental Meditation)

TRUST

What is trust?
Never looking back onto suggestion
and never looking ahead to find a problem.

K.G. Mills (1940±–?)

TRUTH

If it is truth, what does it matter who said it?
Comment: "To those authors I've forgotten, thank you for your words." A.P.

<u>Beauty</u> is the <u>truth</u>,
truth is beauty—
that is all ye need to know on earth
and all ye need to know.
John Keats (1795 1821)

There is nothing so powerful as truth—
and often nothing so strange.
Dave Webster

Adversity is the first path to truth.
Lord George G. N. Byron (1788–1824)

Whatever satisfies the soul is truth.

It always comes back to the same necessity:
go deep enough and there
is a bedrock of truth, however hard.
May Sarton

A <u>sharp mind</u> may find its own <u>truth</u>,
but a humble spirit
finds a truth higher than itself.
Comment: "Age and wisdom should bring humility." A.P.

*The wise man or woman is
he or she who knows how to learn
the truth from every person,
and chooses the truth of each thing.*

The Rebbe (1902–1994) Menachem Mendel Schneerson

TRYING

*If at first you don't succeed,
you're running about average.*

Maxwell H. Anderson (1888–1959)

UNDERSTANDING

*Do not weep; do not wax indignant.
Understand.*

Baruch Spinoza (1632–1677)

UNIVERSAL MESSAGE

*If we are barely awakened,
Wisdom lives in the future,
and from there it speaks to us.*

The Rebbe (1902–1994) Menachem Mendel Schneerson

Comment: "Meditate." A.P.

UNIVERSE

We are not passive observers of this universe;
we are partners in its creation.
We are the ones who
assign each thing its meaning.

The Rebbe (1902–1994) Menachem Mendel Schneerson

Comment: "To Don and Anne Sangster and Herb and Fran Binder, may we continue to share in our children's and our grandchildren's lives." A.P.

VOICE

When the voice is <u>cloaked</u> in feeling,
there is the <u>force</u> to <u>enable change</u>.

K G. Mills (1940±–?)

Comment: "It is not what we say—but how we say it." A.P.

WARMTH

If the world seems cold to you,
kindle fires to warm it.

Lucy Larcom

Comment: "Putting a coat on only warms you—lighting a fire will warm others." A.P.

WEALTH

'Tis the mind that makes the body rich.

He is a wise man
who does not grieve for the things which he has not;
but rejoices for those he has.

Epectetus (55–136 A.D.)

WILL

They can because they think they can.

Virgil (70–19 B.C.)

Comment: "To my granddaughters Jory, Meagan and Rachel—you are capable of *anything,* you will become whatever you put your heart into." A.P.

WINNERS

They can conquer who believe they can.

Ralph Waldo Emerson (1803–1882)

A Winner's Creed

If you think you are beaten, you are;
If you think you dare not, you don't;
If you'd like to win, but think you can't,
It's almost a cinch you won't.
If you think you'll lose, you're lost,
For out in the world we find
Success begins with a fellow's will;
It's all in the state of mind.
If you think you're outclassed, you are;
You've got to think high to rise.
You've got to be sure of yourself before
You can ever win a prize.
Life's battles don't always go
To the stronger or faster man;
But soon or late the man who wins
Is the one who thinks "I can."

Walter D. Wintle

WINNINGS

Winners take chances.

Sammy Davis, Jr. (1925–1990)

The race is not always to the swift,
nor the battle to the strong,
but that's the way to be.

Daymon Runyon (1884–1946)

Comment: "To Mitch and Andrew." A.P.

They will win who believe they can.

Winning is not a sometime thing;
It's an all-time thing.
You don't win once in a while;
you don't do things right once in a while;
you do them right all the time.
Winning is a habit.
Unfortunately, so is losing.

Vince Lombardi (1913–1970)

WINNING

When the One Great Scorer comes
to write against your name,
He marks not that you won or lost,
but how you played the game.

Grantland Rice (1880–1954)

WISDOM

Wisdom entereth not into a malicious mind

Francois Rabelais (1490–1553)

To conquer fear is the beginning of wisdom.

Bertrand Russell (1872–1970)

To my extreme mortification,
I grew wiser every day.
Lord George Byron (1788–1824)

The days that make us happy make us wise.
John Masefield (1878–1967)

A <u>smile</u> is the beginning of wisdom.
Smile and the world smiles with you;
cry and you cry alone.
Comment: "Please keep that beautiful smile Pearl Anne." A.P.

The secret is to become wise before you get old.

Like an ability to move a muscle,
hearing your inner wisdom
is strengthened by doing it.
Robbie Cass, Ph.D., N.D.

A wise man will make
more opportunities than he finds.
Francis Bacon (1561–1626)

Comment: "or woman" A.P.

To have a heart, love.
To have wisdom, cease thinking. Listen.
To have understanding, do.
To have discipline, be <u>willing</u>.
K.G. Mills (1940±–?)

To awaken each morning
with a smile brightening my face;
to greet the day with reverence
for the opportunities it contains;
to approach my work with a clear mind;
to hold ever before me, even in the doing of little things,
the Ultimate Purpose toward which I am working;
to meet men and women
with laughter on my lips and love in my heart;
to be gentle, kind and courteous
through all my hours;
to approach the night with weariness that ever was sleep,
and the joy that comes from work well done—
this is how I desire to waste wisely my days.

Thomas Dekker (1570?–1632)

What is mastership?
Being on the bridge with <u>wisdom</u> and <u>intuition</u>
and allowing <u>insight</u> to scan
the horizon of opportunities.

K.G. Mills (1940±–?)

WOMAN

I am strong; I am invincible; I am woman.

Helen Reddy (1950±–?)

Comment: "Be present at a birth, (as I have 10,000 times),
and then tell me who is the stronger sex." A.P.

WONDER(S)

Wonder opens the windows of your incarceration.

K.G. Mills (1940±–?)

To see a world in a grain of sand,
and heaven in a wild flower,
Hold infinity in the palm of your hand,
and eternity for an hour.

William Blake (1757–1827)

Comment: "This is Naomi's favorite quotation;
Naomi, thank you for Jordan and Adam." A.P.

(*Naomi was my first wife, and the ever beautiful mother of my sons.)

WORLD

The times our generation lives in
are not ordinary times.
We dwell on the interface of two worlds—
a world as it was and
a world as it is meant to be.

The Rebbe (1902–1994) Menachem Mendel Schneerson

WORDS

The words that enlighten the soul
are more precious than jewels.

Hazrat Inayat Khan

Comment: "Benji Merzel speaks with God… and I love speaking with Benji."
(B. Merzel is a chiropractor and a healer who works with our patients.) A.P.

Our words are the camera
that determine our reality;
use them wisely.

The Rebbe (1902–1994) Menachem Mendel Schneerson

The ripple effect of what we say
and what we do—
has greater eternal power
than we could ever possibly imagine.

The Rebbe (1902–1994) Menachem Mendel Schneerson

Comment: "I try each day to remember this, especially when speaking with patients."
A.P.

Speak good words, kind words,
words of wisdom, words of encouragement.
Like gentle rain upon a dormant field.
Eventually, they will coax the seeds
beneath the soil to life.

The Rebbe (1902–1994) Menachem Mendel Schneerson

Comment: "This is part of the origin of my "Thought for the Day"
recorded on my telephone for callers." A.P.

The words on the page are the body
and the ideas behind them are the soul.

The Rebbe (1902–1994) Menachem Mendel Schneerson

It is not always what we say that matters—
but how we say it.

Comment: "Worthy of repeating." A.P.

Words are
a form of action
capable of
influencing change.

Ingrid Bengis (1944–?)

WORK

I will work in my own way,
according to the light that is in me.

Lydia Marie Child (1802–1880)

Comment: "Take the road less travelled... it has made all the difference." A.P.

I know of no more encouraging fact
than the unquestionable ability of man
to elevate his life by conscious endeavor.

Henry David Thoreau (1817–1862)

The victory of success is half won,
when one gains the habit of work.

Sarah A. Bolton (1841–1916)

The secret of happiness is not
in doing what one likes,
but in liking what one has to do.

James M. Barrie (1860–1937)

None preaches better than the ant,
and she says nothing.

Drive thy business;
let not it drive thee.

Comment: "Rationale for my walking away for 6 months in 1994." A.P.

Nothing is really work
unless you would rather be doing something else.

Some men prefer long office hours
because it shortens their hours at home.

The man with time to burn
never gave the world any light.

Absence of occupation is <u>not</u> rest.

*Far and away the best prize that life offers
is the chance to work hard at work worth doing.*
Theodore Roosevelt (1858–1919)
Comment: "Thank you David Garshowitz… your vision will forever change pharmacy. (David Garshowitz is the owner of York Downs Compounding Pharmacy and has been my mentor." A.P.

Laziness shall clothe a man in rags.
Proverbs XXIII:21

*Choose a job you love,
and you will never have to work a day in your life.*
Confucius (551–479 B.C.)
Comment: "I truly love what I do—may G-d grant me more years to do it." A.P.

*The harder you work,
the luckier you get.*
Gary Player (1935–?)

*If there's a job to be done,
I always ask the busiest man in my parish
to take it on,
and it gets done.*
Henry Ward Beecher (1813–1887)

*When love and skill work together,
expect a masterpiece.*
John Ruskin (1819–1900)
Comment: "To my son-in-law, Joel—who I love with all my heart, thank you for all that you have done for this family." A.P.

One thing at a time,
and all things in succession,
That which grows slowly,
endures.

Josiah G. Holland (1819–1881)

Comment: "To Mathew—find your place in the sun and you will shine." A.P.

How to make your wit and your width to swell?
Do one thing at a time, and do it well.

John Stuart Blackie (1809–1895)

Good order is the foundation of all good things.

Edmund Burke (1729–1797)

WORRY

We are perhaps unique among
the earth's creatures: the worrying animal.
We worry away our lives, fearing the future,
discontent with the present, unable to take in
the idea of dying, unable to sit still.

Lewis Thomas

Comment: "Monday morning at 9:00 A.M. is the most common time
for someone to have a heart attack in North America." A.P.

Awareness shows that, miraculously,
the universe (and all the people in it)—
continue to function without my worry.

Hugh Prather (1945±–?)

Comment: "Don't worry my darling Carol, everything that love touches will find its way—our children and their children will *always* know the power of your love." A.P.

WRITING

Nothing contributes so much to
tranquilize the mind as a steady purpose,
a point on which the soul
may fix its intellectual eye.

Mary Shelley (1797–1851)

A little knowledge that acts
is worth infinitely more
than much knowledge that is idle.

Kahlil Gibran, the Prophet (1883–1931)

The differing nature of day and night
can't be explained by the absence of light.
Something moves at night.
There is a presence.
The demons come out,
but so do the muses.

Comment: "I write at night." A.P.

Night is the mother of thoughts.

John Florio (1553–1626)

<u>*Words*</u> *are the* <u>*only things*</u> *that* <u>*last forever*</u>.

Comment: "May some of these words last with you—take care of each other." A.P.

Alvin Pettle

M.D. FRCS(C)

ADAMS, Henry (Henry Brooks Adams) (1838–1918) American (USA) historian, author; wrote *History of the United States from 1801 to 1817* (1889–1891); works on the European Middle Ages and *The Education of Henry Adams* (1918). *See:* **Teacher**

ADDISON, Joseph, B.A., M.A. (1672–1719) English; Statesman, known for Latin poetry and prose; Christian; trilingual (English/French/Latin), both degrees from Oxford University, Fellow of Queen's College, Oxford (1698); best known for *An Account of the Greatest English Poets* (except); *A Letter from Italy* and *Ode*. *See:* **Reading**.

ANDERSON, Maxwell H. (1888–1959) American (USA) playwright: comedy *What Price Glory?* (1929); historical plays *Elizabeth the Queen* (1930) and satire *Both Your Houses* (1933) and two poetic plays with a contemporary setting, *Winterset* (1934) and *High Tor* (1936). *See:* **Trying**

ARTISTOTLE, (384–322 B.C.) Greek; philosopher; son of the court physician to King Amyntas of Macedonia; his father dying young, he was sent at age 17 to Athens, then the intellectual centre of the world, to complete his education; pupil of Plato for 20 years, tutor of Alexander of Macedonia (at ages 13–18) who later became Alexander the Great (world conqueror); founded Peripatetic School of Athens (335 B.C.) In 344; as Aristotle had a habit of walking about when he lectured, his followers became known as the "peripatetics," meaning "to walk about"; he was renowned for his rhetoric (language skills, especially to convince others); his philosophy was concerned with logic (which he termed verbal reasoning), idealism, science and phenomena of the world; ethics was for him "an attempt to find our chief end or highest good," he was known for original, profound analyses which had enormous influence on subsequent philosophical thought and understanding; best known for *Organon* (logic), *Ethics, Politics, Poetics, On the Soul* (biographical); *Metaphysics* and *Historia Animalium*. *See:* **Addiction**

ARMSTRONG, Louis (Louis Daniel Armstrong) nickname "Satchmo," short for "Satchel Mouth" (1901–1971) American (USA) jazz trumpet player/soloist, singer (known for his distinctive gravely voice) writer (lyrics and prose) and actor (30 films): considered the founder of jazz, a uniquely American art form; performed for 50 years, an average of 300 concerts a year for several decades, wrote lyrics for dozens of songs (including *"Hello, Dolly,"* and *"It's a Wonderful World,"* always known for his bubbly personality and perfect comedic timing, on-stage and off. Example of the American "rags to riches" life, he was born in very poor section of New Orleans known as the "Battlefield"; at 12 was sent to a reform school for 2 years for firing off a gun on New Year's Eve, but where he learned to play coronet, on his release was too poor to buy an instrument until given one by Joe "King" Oliver, into whose jazz band he started to play horns as a regular member by 1917 (age 16); he possessed natural perfect pitch and, it was said, a perfect sense of rhythm, and was known for his always original improvisations in melodies and vocals, Wrote 2 autobiographies, plus scores of magazine articles, memoirs and thousands of letters; *See:* **Life**

BACON, Francis, Baron Verulam of Verulam, Viscount St. Albans (1561–1626), English statesman, author and essayist; credited with laying down the first classification of natural sciences and created a new inductive method of reasoning in philosophy. *The Essays* (1597) are his chief literary work, his incomplete *Instatauratio* was an attempt to reorganize the entire body of human knowledge to that time. Distinguished parliamentarian under Elizabeth I, James I and became Chancellor (1618) but lost his office in 1621 after being accused of taking bribes. *See:* **Ego, Wisdom**

BANKS, George Linnaeus (1821–1881) English writer, poet, journalist, play-wright, lyricist, editor; born in Birmingham; after trying a few trades, at the age of 17 contributed to various newspapers and became a journalist, subsequently a playwright, writing burlesques and 2 plays, as well as lyrics for several songs; edited a succession of newspapers, including the Birmingham Mercury (England) and the Dublin Daily Express (Ireland), published several volumes of miscellaneous prose and verse. *See:* **Life**

BARRIE, James M. (Sir James Matthew Barrie) (1860–1937) Scottish novelist, dramatist, playwright; born the ninth child of a weaver and the daughter of a stonemason, educated at Dumfries Academy and Edinburgh University; first a journalist in Nottingham

(England), then a novelist, then a playwright, including *Quality Stret, What Every Woman Knows* and *The Admirable Crichton,* but he will be remembered mainly for his fantasy play, *Peter Pan,* about a boy who wouldn't grow up and creates his own world of Indians, pirates and fairies, first produced in 1904, adapted with music in 1950, as a musical play in 1954, revived in 1979, made into film (silent in 1924) and feature length cartoon animated (1952); he devoted all his rights in *Peter Pan* to a local children's hospital; elected Chancellor of Edinburgh University (1930–1937). *See:* **Work**

BEECHER, Henry Ward (1813–1887) American (USA) clerical leader, writer and political activist; spokesman for the Protestantism (Christian) of his time; his sermons in the 1850s at Plymouth Church in Brooklyn, New York won him the largest congregation in the USA. He was a fervent advocate of the emancipation of slaves and of women's suffrage (right to vote). *See:* **Work**

BELLOC, Hilaire (Joseph Hilaire Pierre Belloc) (1870–1953) English Roman Catholic Christian (born in France) author, satirist, journalist, editor, historian, newspaper publisher, parliamentarian, activist; became a citizen of Britain (1902); a Liberal member of Parliament (1906–1910); among his works best remembered for *The Bad Child's Book of Beasts* (1896); *Marie Antoinette* (1910) and *Napoleon* (1922); a close friend of author G.K. Chesterton, together they founded the *New Witness,* a weekly political newspaper and invested and propagated Distributism, an anti-capitalist, anti-Fabian socialist philosophy. *See:* **Life**

BENGIS, Ingrid (1944–?), American (USA) author, born the daughter of Russian immigrants, she grew up wondering if she was American or Russian; In 1991, settled in St. Petersburg, Russia about which she wrote *Metro Stop Doestoevsky, Travels in Russian Time,* an exploration of what life was like at the turn of the millennium (1999–2000), a period of immense turmoil in Russia, exploring in Russian fashion the centuries-old preoccupation with "the big questions," tradition and progress, destiny and activism, scepticism and faith. Also authored *Man-Hating, Combat in the Erogenous Zone,* a finalist for the 1972 USA National Book Award and a novel, *I Have Come Here to Be Alone;* Lives now in Maine, USA and St. Petersburg, Russia. *See:* **Words**

BERATH, Mary Wolston *See:* Sex

BERGSON, Henri (1859–1941) French philosopher, professor (science and mathematics) and key early thinker in the existentialist current; Jewish; Born in Paris, Polish/Irish parents, spent his early years in London, England, until age 9, when his parents returned to France. He held the prestigious chair of modern philosophy at the College de France from 1900 to 1921; was awarded an honorary Doctor of Letters by Cambridge University in 1920; awarded the Nobel Prize for Literature in 1927. His philosophy generally emphasized opposition between human creativity (rooted in life and the inner stream of consciousness) and spatial objectifications of experience (in stable cultural forms and institutions). His numerous writings included *Time and Free Will, Matter and Memory, Creative Evolution* and *Two Sources of Morality and Religion. See:* **Personality**

BISMARCK (Prince Otto Eduard Leopold von Bismarck) (1815–1898) German statesman (1862–1890). Born a Prussian junker (a member of the aristocratic, formerly privileged class) in Prussia, which was the largest German sub-state with a population in 1939 of 41 million, the Prussian people having a history from the 10th century until 1945 (end of World War II) when it was divided among war victors, first appointed Chancellor in 1862 by Wilhelm I; invaded and conquered Austria in The Seven Weeks War (1866); precipitated Franco-Prussian war (1870–71); First Chancellor of the German Reich (1871), known for his social reforms, protective tariffs, and colonial policies fostering trade and industry. Friction with Wilhelm II led to his dismissal (1890). *See:* **Children**

BLACK, CLAUDIA, M.S.W., Ph.D, (Contemporary 1960±–?) American (USA) psychologist, crisis counsellor, and self-help motivational author of many books including: *Family Secrets; Life Stories of Adult Children of Alcoholics* (1987); *It Will Never Happen To Me* (1991), *The Missing Piece; Solving the Puzzle of Self* (1995), *Changing Course, Healing from Loss, Abandonment and Fear* (1999), and *What Parents Should Tell Their Kids about Drugs and Alcohol* (2003). *See:* **Respect, Self, Self-Care**

BLACKIE, John Stuart, Dr., L.L.B. (1809–1895) Scottish; one of the best-known of his countrymen at his time; lawyer, professor, lecturer, educational reformer, writer; music historian; born and educated to B.A. in Aberdeen (Scotland), then three years at the Universities of Göttingen and Berlin (both Germany) and Rome (Italy) which made him highly multilingual (English, German, Italian, Greek) and gave him a life-long love of the German language and culture and the Greek language and antiquity; then back to Edinburgh (Scotland) for a law degree; member of the Scottish bar (law); also Professor of Humanities (Aberdeen); then Chair of Greek at the University of Edinburgh; his books include: *War Songs of the Germans* (1879), *Scottish Song* (1889), *The Scottish Students' Song Book* (1891); he was a charismatic lecturer in many subjects, promoted educational reform and the Gaelic language; raised funds and created the Chair of Celtic at Edinburgh University; was so loved by the Scottish people that the day of his funeral was declared a national day of mourning and the City of Edinburgh and its citizens halted entirely to attend his funeral. *See:* **Doubt, Success, Work**

BLAKE, William (1757–1827) English poet, writer (prose), painter (water-colors), professional engraver and mystic; early works *Songs of Innocence* (1789) and *Songs of Experience* (1794) were considered lyrical with some symbolism but his later works *Milton* (1804–08) and *Jerusalem* (1804–20) were considered entirely symbolic; most of his books were self-manufactured with his own original process of "illuminated printing," text and pictures done in reverse on metal with acid-proof ink, then treated with acid, printed by hand and hand-colored; also known for his engravings and illustrations from several additional books; a considerable number of his poems were set to music for Christian Protestant congregations. *See:* **Doubt, Success, Wonder(s)**

BOLTON, Sarah K. (1841–1916) American (USA) writer, teacher, suffragette (advocate of women's right to vote), temperance and reform movement worker, including animal rights; born in Connecticut, descended from one of the 26 original incorporators of the Massachusetts Bay Colony; met activist Harriet Beecher Stowe (age 11, in 1852); educated at Hartford Female Seminary; traveled in Europe studying women's education and labor conditions (1881–1883; first published at the age of 15; taught school in Natchez,

Mississippi until the outbreak of the Civil War (1861); Associate Editor of the *Congregationalist*, maintained a writing career which embraced poetry, children's literature and biographies (1864–1902); her writings reflect her belief in the ability to better one's world through faith and hard work. *See:* **Work**

BOUEE, Christian *See:* **Faith**

BONAPARTE, NAPOLEON; *See NAPOLEON, BONAPARTE (this list); See:* **Harm**

BRAYCETT, Berton *See:* **Praise**

BRIAND, Aristide (1862–1932) French socialist statesman, 10 times prime Minister between 1909 and 1929; took a leading part in bringing about the separation of church and state (1905), formation of the League of Nations and signing of the Locarno Pact (1925) and the Kellogg-Briand Pact (1928); an early advocate of a federal European union. *See:* **Adversity**

BRIDGES, William (Bill), Ph.D. (Contemporary 1950±–?) American (USA) motivational psychologist, speaker, executive and personal development coach, career and life planning consultant and author who helps individuals and organizations deal productively with change; considered the world's leading authority in managing transitions; earned his B.A. from Harvard University, his M.A. from Columbia and Ph.D. from Brown University; has written 9 books, the first now in its 35th printing, *Transitions: Making Sense of Life's Changes* (1980); his most recent book is *Job Shift: How to Prosper in a Workplace Without Jobs*, which has been translated into 8 languages; past president of the Association for Humanistic Psychology. *See:* **Opportunity**

BRISTOL, Claude M. (1891–1951) American (USA) motivational author, books include *The Magic of Believing* (1969) and *TNT-The Power Within You* (1982) *See:* **Dreams**

BROOKS, Mel (Melvin Kaminsky) (1926–?) American (USA) stand-up comic, actor, comedy writer, director and producer, investor, businessman; born in Brooklyn, New York; best known as creator of broad film farces and paradies; co-created TV series *Get Smart*, 12 films include *Young Frankensein* and *Blazing Saddles*, both of which he wrote and directed in 1974. In 2002, he transferred his film, *The Producers*, to the Broadway stage. One of a rare group who has received an Oscar, twice an Emmy (as both an actor and writer), a Tony and a Grammy. Married to actress, Anne Bancroft, maintains homes in New York and California. *See:* **Death**

BROOKS, Philips (Bishop of Massachusetts) (1835–1893) American (USA) clergyman (Episcopal Christian, Bishop), orator, advocate for emancipation (end of slavery), writer of books, hymns and poems; born in Boston, Massachusetts, proud descendant of early Puritans; raised in a religious household, where his parents held hymn-sings on Sunday evenings, he knew 200 hymns by memory by the time he went to college; studied at Harvard; ordained 5 years before the American Civil War began; considered one of the more eloquent speakers of his time, with a rapid delivery, he preached in leading Boston and Philadelphia churches, defending the idea of God in Three Persons; chosen Bishop in 1891; published many books including *Lectures on Preaching* (1877) and *Sermons Preached in English Churches* (1883); best remembered by many for writing the lyrics to the hymn *O Little Town of Bethlehem* (1868). His tomb reads: "A preacher of righteousness in utterance, rejoicing in the truth, unhampered by the bonds of church or state, he brought by his life and doctrine fresh faith to a people, fresh meanings to ancient creeds." *See:* **Life**

BROWN, Les, Ph.D. (1912–2001) American (USA) big band leader. during the 1940s and 1950s. Received his degree in music from Ithica Conservatory of Music, Ithica, New York State, graduated Valedictorian at New York Military Academy and attended Duke University. Began as a freelance music arranger (for Jimmy Dorsey, among others). His band, the Band of Renown, was formed in 1938, which featured vocalist Doris Day, remembered for their recording of *Sentimental Journey* in 1945 (the year World War II ended). Produced many music recordings, tapes and CDs. Was music director for numerous

TV specials including 18 overseas tours with Bob Hope, the *Steve Allen TV* show, the *Dean Martin TV* show and *Swing Love* (1996) TV. Guest conductor for many symphonies, including the United States Air Force Band many times. Received honorary Doctorate of Music from Ithaca Conservatory of Music. In 1996, his band was entered into Guinness Book of World Records as "Longest Organized Group in the History of Popular Music." Died of lung cancer. *See:* **Aspiration**

BROWNING, Robert (1812–1889) English romantic poet, writer, monologist. His dramatic monologues (a style in which he was considered to have no rival) are astute studies of personality; noted for his expressions of tenderness, compassion and love, particularly in his poetry; in his book *The Ring and the Book* (1868–9), he tells the same story 12 times, each from the point of view of a different character; married to noted author Elizabeth Barrett Browning. *See:* **Aspirations**

BRYAN, William Jennings (1860–1925) American (usa) Fundamentalist Protestant Christian; northern politician, noted orator; unsuccessfully ran for u.s. president (1896, 1900 and 1908); appointed Secretary of State by President Woodrow Wilson; resigned (1915) when Wilson protested to Germany over sinking of u.s. *Lusitainia*; proposed progressive measures including depression relief to agriculture and industry, popular election of senators, imposition of an income tax act and women's suffrage (right to vote); as an opponent of Darwinism, helped to prosecute (and lose) famous case against teaching Darwin's theory of evolution in u.s. (Tennessee) elementary schools, the Scopes Trial (1925) *See:* **Destiny**

BRYANT, Bear (Coach) (1913–1983) American (usa) football coach, born Moro Bottom, Arkansas, the son of modest share-cropping farmers. After playing on the Rose-Bowl winning 1935 University of Alabama team, he coached for 38 years at 4 southern universities. At Alabama (1958–82), he "Crimson Tide" teams won or shared six national championships. He retired with 323 wins, the record for coaches in the top-rated Division 1-A. *See:* **Courage**

BUDDHA (Prince Guatama Siddhartha) (563–483 B.C.) Indian founder of Buddhism (known as "the Englightened One"); religious founder; son of a rajah of the Sakya tribe ruling in Kapilvistu, Nepal, member of the Kahatriya caste, born near the present borders of India and Nepal. Raised in extreme luxury and protected from harsh experiences, at the age of 30 he met adversity for the first time, in the forms of a senile old man, a sick man, a corpse and a wandering ascetic (a person who practices severe denial of self for religious reasons) after which he left his luxurious court, his beautiful wife and all earthly possessions, became a rigorous ascetic for 6 years, then according to tradition achieved enlightenment through deep meditation and began to teach for the next 45 years, gaining many disciples, founding a school for them; and died at about the age of 80. He is regarded as a naturalistic atheist by many disciples and analysts. Buddhism has 500 million adherents, mostly in Asia. *See also* **SANSKRIT** *in this list. See:* **Health**

BUMPER STICKER, *observed in Toronto in the 1960s: See:* **Death**

BURKE, Edmund (1729–1797) Irish, British statesman, politician, writer and conservative political theorist; opposed George III's personal rule, defending parliamentary government; supported the American colonies in their fight (1775–83) for independence; attacked legal abuses and the slave trade; exposed injustices in India; advocate of many practical reforms, he feared political reform; opposed the French Revolution (1790); was considered a master pamphleteer/propagandist. *See:* **Work**

BURKE, Leo J. *See:* **Babies**

BURTON, Robert (who used the pseudonym Democritus Junior) (1577–1640) English writer; vicar (Church of England, Christian) reformer; studied at Oxford University, his epic *Anatomy of Melancholy* first published in 1621 was republished 7 times further in the 1600s and then not again until 1800, then once again in 1932, 1989–94 and 2001; considered by many critics as a staggering extensive compendium (1392 pages) of authoritative excepts and quotations from every important book every written or published on literature, sciences, medicine, astronomy, philosophy, politics, nature, all the arts and melancholia up to that date (1621), in which he quoted earlier scientific, historical, philosophical and spiritual arguments from virtually all important preceding authorities, from the earliest Greek to his recent contemporaries, consisting almost entirely of quotes and references to the thoughts of others, woven together into a tapestry with which he proceeded to argue and amplify his own opinions, to educate and provide inspiration to fellow suffers of melancholia (depression); still used as a reference source nearly 400 years later; considered by modern critics as a meta-fictional challenge far greater than any undertaken by any other writer for centuries later; his arguments appear to be that the soul and conscience are an integral part of a human being, and that man is built, at least in terms of brain function, literally in the image of God. *See:* **Meditation**

BYRON, Lord (George Gordon Noel Byron, 6th Baron) (1788–1824) English romantic poet, satirist, writer; ultimate example of the romantic in his irregular personal life and emotion-charged poetry; lame from birth, left fatherless (1791), he grew to be a dark handsme man, beloved by and contemptuous of women; he was linked with various women both before and after his ill-fated marriage (1815–16) to Anne Isabella Milbanke; restlessly wandering about the Continent and while working for Greek independence, he wrote long romances and stories in verse such as *Childe Harold* (1812–18), *Manfred* (1817) and *Cain* (1820); much criticized for his skepticism towards religion, he was a master of satire, as in *English Bards and Scotch Reviewers* (1809) and his masterpiece *Don Juan* (1819–24); also wrote many other short and longer pieces. *See:* **Wisdom**

CADDY, Eileen (1930–?) American (USA) spiritual writer who with her husband and two friends founded Findhorn, a non-denominational religious retreat in Scotland, on the Moray Firth near Royal Air Force Base Kinloss. *See:* **Expectations**

CANTOR, Eddie, Edward Israel Iskowitzt (1910–1964) American (USA) singer and radio show host of a comedy-variety show featuring vaudeville and burlesque from 1931 to 1949. Born to Russian immigrants, both of whom died soon after his birth, he grew up poor, living in tenement houses in New York city with his grandmother. When he reached school, the registrar misspelled his name "Kanter" which he later changed to

"Cantor." A frequent truant, hooligan and petty thief, he also discovered a natural talent for singing. Starting his career as a singing waiter on Coney Island, he met Jimmy Durante, who was the restaurant's pianist. He later appeared on Rudy Vallee's "Fleischmann Hour" and then the "Chase and Sanborn Show" which was renamed "the Eddy Cantor Show" to keep him on the show. During its run, the show was known for many publicity stunts, including declaring Eddy Cantor a candidate for President, for which he received many write-in votes. *See:* **Life**

CAPTA, Fritjof, Physicist *See:* **Insight**

CASALS, Pablo (1876–1973) Spanish virtuoso cellist, conductor and composer, first toured widely internationally with the cello in a trio (with piano and violin), in 1919 formed Orchestra Pau Casals in Barcelona, but left Spain to protest Francisco Franco's regime; spent his latter life in the USA, associated with the Marlboro Music Festival in Vermont; composed El Pessebre (*The Manger*), a sacred oratorio (1960); toured widely around the world as cello soloist and conductor, recording artist. *See:* **Death**

CASS, Robbie, PH.D., N.D., (Contemporary) American (USA) scientist, naturopathic doctor *See:* **Wisdom**

CEOS *See:* **Appearance**

CERVANTES, Miguel De (1547–1616) Spanish author and dramatist, whose best known work is *Don Quixote* (1605), a novel episodic in structure with many inserted stories, the hero of which is a parody of the knight errant and at the same time a perfect exponent of chivalric nobility remembered most commonly as tilting at windmills. *See:* **Courage, Desire, Preparation**

CHAMFORT, N. (Sebastien Roch Nicholas Chamfort) (1740–1794) French, writer of maxims and epigrams, a savage critic of society and a republican, he was favored by the French court and as a member of the upper class was persecuted under the French

Revolution. (Many historians believe the major reason for the Revolution was the bankruptcy of the French government after widespread wars in the two previous centuries and gross mismanagement by the bureaucracy, resulting in gross over-taxation, hardship and lack of food and necessities for the citizens; the Revolution began in 1789 and only ended by Napoleon Bonaparte's coup d'etat in 1799; during its course; Tribunals of common citizens, amid widespread intrigues, corruption, run-away inflation and bankruptcies, mercilessly persecuted the court and upper classes whom they held responsible for the economic devastation, famine and universal misery of the country); Chamfort committed suicide (at age 54) to escape the guillotine. *See:* **Laughter, Passion**

CHILD, Lydia Maria (1802–1880) American (USA) novelist, poet, story-writer, schoolteacher, editor, writer for children and confrontationist. Her first notorious novel was *Hobomok, a Tale of Early Times* (1824) which celebrated inter-racial marriage. Later, she published books for an on women, including among others: *The Frugal Housewife* (1829), *The History of the Condition of Women* (1935), *Juvenile Miscellany* (1826–1834) in which was some of her most memorable poetry; *An Appeal in Favour of That Class of Americans Called Africans* (1833) and editorship of the *National Anti-Slavery Standard* (1841–43) established her as an abolitionist (against slavery); poetry collections included *Flowers for Children* (3 volumes), *Autumnal Leaves* and *Looking Towards Sunset*, married in 1828 to David Lee Child until his death (1874) and lived in Wayland, Massachusetts. *See:* **Work**

CHINESE PROVERB (500 B.C.) most Chinese proverbs originate with Confucius and Confucianism, and became part of the folklore and oral tradition of the Chinese people, who comprise almost ⅓ of the world's population world-wide, for nearly 2,000 years until the 1900s when Mao Tse-Tung founded the Communist party in China (1921), introduced the Chinese Cultural Revolution (1966) and over the next few decades transformed China to a Communist country (non-religious); Communism espousing as per the teachings of Karl Marx that property and other forms of wealth be owned by the whole of a classless society, with wealth shared on the principle of "to each according to his need," each yielding fully according to his ability to contribute to the common good; in practice, the Proverbs continued as part of the ongoing oral history and inspiration of the Chinese people, although frequently attributed to contemporary political leaders *See also* CONFUCIUS *and* TSE, LAO *in this list. See:* Enemies

CHURCHILL, Winston, Sir (William Leonard Spencer Churchill) (1874–1965) British leader, statesman, parliamentarian, orator, soldier, journalist, writer, historian, painter; born in Blenheim Palace, near Oxford, England, son of Lord Randolph Churchill and American (USA) on his mother's side, through whom he was one-eighth Iroquois Indian; graduate of the Royal Military College at Sandhurst, soldier and journalist in Cuba, India, Egypt and South Africa; as parliamentarian took a leading part in laying the foundations of the welfare state in Britain, preparing the Royal Navy for World War I, as Prime Minister of Britain during most of World War II emerged as the inspired leader of the united British nation and Commonwealth countries and allies to resist German domination of Europe; considered a master radio orator, inspiring resistance among his people and a prime architect of victory in World War II. His career is considered the most prestigious in British history for richness, range, length and achievement; his dominant qualities were relentless courage, optimism, imagination, humor, as well as a powerful, original and fertile intellect; in addition to active journalism, he wrote many books including *A History of the English Speaking Peoples,* 4 volumes (1933–1939), received the Nobel Prize for Literature in 1953, resigned as Prime Minister in his 80th year but continued to sit in Parliament until his 89th year, in addition to knighthood by the Queen of England, in 1963 by special act of the U.S. Congress, he was made an honorary American (USA) citizen. *See:* Responsibility

CIDE, André *See:* Discovery

CLEMENS, Samuel Longhorne *(See instead: Mark TWAIN is this list)*

COLETTE, pen name of (Sidonie Gabrielle Claudine Colette de Jouvenel) (1873–?) French romantic novelist, famous (and somewhat scandalous) for analytical psychological studies of women, in particular *Cheri* (1920, English translation 1929) in which an aging courtesan has an affair with the son of a friend and *La Chatte* (1933, English translation 1936); with her first husband, Willy (pseudonymn of Henri Gauthier-Villars), she collaborated on the famous *Claudine* stories. *See:* **Mistakes**

COLY, R. *See:* **Addiction**

CONANT, James Bryant (1893–1978) American (USA) chemist; educator, administrator, diplomat; Professor of Organic Chemistry, Harvard (1929–1933), appointed President of Harvard University (1933), Chairman of the National Defense Research Committee (942–45), appointed USA High Commissioner for Germany (1953) and Ambassador to Germany (1955–57). *See:* **Chance**

CONFUCIUS (551–479 B.C.) Chinese philosopher and founder of a religion bearing his name, Confucianism; born Kong Qiu in the state of Lu (in Shandong), spent 15 years of his adult life as a public administrator, then spent the rest studying and teaching the classics; Confucianism becoming the predominant moral and ethical system of China for 2500 years until mid-1900s when Communism prevailed (population of China 1½ billion); his original sayings called the *Anelects* were recorded after his death and edited by disciples in various points in history thereafter. Basically, it is a system of ethical precepts, benevolent love, righteousness, decorum, wise leadership, sincerity, the good management of family and society. *See:* **Enemies, Forgiveness, Work**

COPELAND, Aaron (1900–1990) American (USA) musician, solo pianist, composer (orchestral music, ballet, opera, film, chamber, solo piano and vocal), conductor, write; born in Brooklyn, New York; one of five children, his father a department store owner; he completed High School at age 18 and decided not to go to college but to devote his life to music; studied in New York and went to France, at age 21, for further study in Paris; devoted his life as a composer to creating, fostering, developing and establishing a distinctive "American" music and became known as the "Dean of American Music; by 1925, his first *Symphony for Organ and Orchestra* (1924) was performed by the New York Philharmonic; thereafter composed a major body of music and writing; became head of the Composition Department of the Juilliard School of Music when it opened (1924), received a Guggenheim Memorial Fellowship (1925–26) and (1926–27); taught composition at Harvard University (1935); wrote first ballet *Billy the Kid* (1938); wrote first of four books *What to Listen for in Music* (1939); taught composition at Tanglewood, Massachusetts (1940); toured Latin America several times; completed *Lincoln Portrait* (1942), the ballet *Rodeo* (1942) and *Fanfare for the Common Man* (1942); completed composition *Appalachian Spring* and won the Pulitzer Price for Music (1945); received Medal of Freedom from President of U.S. "highest civil honor for service in peacetime"; received Kennedy Center Honors (1979) and many other national awards. *See:* **Self-Consciousness**

COUSE, Emile (1875–1926) *See:* **Improvement**

COUSINS, Norman (1915–1990) American (USA) psychologist, motivational speaker, seminar leader and inspirational and motivational writer; editor *See:* **Laughter**

CROCKETT, Davy (Colonel) (1786–1836) American (USA) backwoods statesman, soldier, bear-hunter, Indian-fighter and celebrated Tennessee sharpshooter best known as a hero who died, as one of 189 martyrs, in defense of the Alamo (Texas) against a large Mexican army (over 2,000 of whom were also killed in the same battle) in the U.S. war to liberate Texas from Mexico (1836). His grandparents were massacred by Creek and Cherokee Indians in 1777; later his father was a log-cabin tavern operator on the Tennessee Knoxville-Abingdon Road, (which was much traveled by settlers heading west to land offered free to homesteaders in the western territories). While quite young, he lasted four days in school, and the second time he tried, as a young teenager he lasted six months. That was his only formal schooling, yet he was awarded rank as a colonel, served as a commander of a battalion in the Creek Indian War of 1813–14, was a member of the Tennessee legislature (1821–1929), and then a member of Congress of the USA for Tennessee (1829–1931 and 1833–35). *See:* **Confidence**

CURTIS, G. W. (George William Curtis) (1824–1892) American (USA) author, editor and orator, administrator, reformer; his most popular book was a series of essays, *Prue and I* (1856); was long one of the editors of the magazines *Harper's Monthly* and *Harper's Weekly;*

*c*ampaigned for emancipation (against slavery) and for civil service reform and woman's suffrage (right to vote); Chancellor of New York University 1890–92. *See:* **Books**

DAVIS, Sammy (Jr.) (1925–1990), American (USA) Jewish Black entertainer, singer, tap-dancer, comedian, actor; born to the stage (had traveled 10 states and played 50 cities by age 4 in a vaudeville family); rags to riches story; child film star in *Rufus Jones for President* about a little black boy who falls asleep in his mother's lap and dreams he is president; endured major episodes of anti-racial prejudice in his youth and during army service; wrote several books including his memoir *Yes I Can* (1965) and *Why Me?* (1980); converted to Judaism in mid-life; had extensive successful career in films, stage and as a touring entertainer, including Las Vegas; close personal friendships with Frank Sinatra, Dean Martin, Jerry Lewis, Elvis Presley Hugh Hefner and the Kennedy presidential family; well remembered for his number one single *Candy Man* which was a song he called horrible; died of throat cancer. at age 65. *See:* **Winning**

DEKKER, Thomas (1570?–1632) English poet, writer, dramatist and pamphleteer/pro-pagandist; resident of London, *The Shoemaker's Holiday,* his best known play and *The Gull's Hornbook* (1608) his most famous prose work, show his understanding of London life and people, humorous satire and vigorous style. *See:* **Wisdom**

DELACROIX, Eugene (Ferdinand Victor Eugene Delacroix) (1798–1863) French painter (landscape and portraits); the leader of the Romantic school; consciously rejected clas-sical formal elements; his composition is free and turbulent; his colors powerful and an essential part of the picture's structure; found his inspirations in exotic subjects: Arab life, fierce wild animals, warfare; excellent portrait painter; his *Journal* is a source of romantic ideas. *See:* **Inspiration**

DE MILLE, Agnes (Agnes de Mille) (1909–1993) American (USA); concert dancer, cho-reographer of Broadway musical stage shows, ballets, teacher of dance, founder and principal of dance school, writer, lecturer; born in Harlem, New York City, New York of a famous and successful stage family (including her uncle, legendary Hollywood director Cecil B. de Mille); knew she wanted to be a dancer by age 5; at age 12, she saw the legendary ballerina Anna Pavlova dance and was inspired to study and make a career of ballet and dance; studied at University of Southern California; studied and danced as a soloist in England and Europe; remembered by friends and family for her extraordinary energy and mass of red hair, by the public for her innovative choreographic routines in musical stage shows: the first, *Black Ritual*, with an all American black cast (1940), *Rodeo* (1942) and *Fall River Legend* (1948); in musical shows on Broadway, she is credited with changing ballet in modern musical theatre by bringing American folklore to ballet, beginning with *Oklahoma* (1943), then *Carousel, Gentlemen Prefer Blonde, Paint Your Wagon* and *110 in the Shade;* she was also a prolific writer of books about dance and dancers and wrote for many publications; won many awards including the Kennedy Honors (1980); was still lecturing until she died of a stroke and heart disease at age 89. *See:* **Silence**

DICKINSON, Emily (1830–1886) American (USA) poet; an unmarried intense recluse, and was virtually unknown in her time; daughter of a lawyer; published only seven of her 2000 poems during her lifetime; after her death several hundred were edited and published by her friends in three volumes, but frequently were significantly different from her original writing; most was published within the last 75 years (after (1925) by Harvard University Press; she wrote mainly of death and immortality in short, intense, mostly unrhymed lyrics, in which the skillful use of assonace (informal, partial rhyme wherein the vowels are alike but the consonants are different) often gives the illusion of rhyme. (1804–1881) *See:* **Living**

DISRAELI, Benjamin, 1st Earl of Beaconsfield (1804–1881) British statesman, parliamentarian and novelist; prime minister 1868 and 1874–80; born Jewish, he was baptized Anglican in 1817; gained reputation as novelist with *Vivian Grey* (1826) and entered parliament (1837); his political views based on aristocracy, the queen and the Church are expressed in his novels *Coningsby* (1844) and *Sybyl* (1845); got the Reform Bill passed (giving the vote to all householders); as Prime Minister (1874–80) he was noted for his tact, declaring Queen Victoria as Empress of India (1877); his vigorous foreign policy included purchasing on his own behalf an interest in the Suez Canal (1875); colonial failures in

Afghanistan and South Africa contributed to his electoral defeat (1880) to his life-long political rival, William Gladstone. *See:* **Determination, Grief**

DOUGLAS, Norman (1868–1952) Austrian novelist, essayist, antiquary (student or collector of relics from ancient times), autobiographer, editor, geologist, historian, humorist, literary critic, pamphleteer/propagandist, scientist, story and travel writer, zoologist; born into a predominantly Scottish family who were in Austria to run cotton mills; aged 5 when his father died; attended British schools which he hated and transferred to Baden, Germany where he studied widely, mastering several languages; first published article on natural history when he was 17; spent much of his life in Italy, but traveled the Continent; accused of child molestation in 1916, he fled England to escape trial; wrote many books, the most successful of which were a novel, *South Wind* (1917), and several travel books on Italy, *Old Calabria*, and Austria; produced an autobiography *Looking Back* in 1933; another scandal forced him to flee Italy in 1937, only returning to that country in 1946. He apparently committed suicide fulfilling his own comment, "Why prolong life save to prolong pleasure?" His works reflect his wit, unapologetic hedonism and reverence for the physical world. *See:* **Experience**

DRYDEN, John (1631–1700) English poet, dramatist and critic; first came to note with *Heroick Stanzas* (1659), commemorating Oliver Cromwell but welcomed Charles II with *Astraea Redux* and rose to prominence in the Restoration; was made Poet Laureate (1862); converted to Roman Catholicism and on the accession of William III lost the Poet Laureate position and court patronage but remained prominent; wrote many long poems including *MacFlecknoe* (1682, a satirical attack); two of his best-known shorter pieces are *Ode to the Memory of Mrs. Anne Killigrew*, and *Alexander's Feast;* he also wrote many shorter poems and plays (comedies and tragedies); his work was much admired for its style and he also wrote brilliant critical prefaces, prologues and discourses; also known for translating and adapting much Latin literature. *See:* **Mind(s)**

DWIGHT, John Sullivan, Dr. (1813–1893) American (USA), Unitarian theologian, Trancendentalist, lecturer, teacher, first influential American classical music critic; music historian, music teacher, producer of musicals and theatrical events, writer, translator of *Select Minor Poems of Goethe and Schiller* from German; upholder of Bach, Handel and Beethoven's music; born in Boston, educated at Harvard Divinity School, graduated in 1836; visited Europe for 17 months in 1860; Director of Brook Farm School, a commune dedicated to farming and providing a more simple and wholesome life where he taught for 5 years Latin, Green, German and music; wrote regular columns on music for many publications; friend of Ralph Waldo Emerson; his best known original poem was *God Save the State. See:* **Rest**

EARHART, Amelia (1898–1937) American (usa) aviation pioneer, pilot of solo engine airplanes, the first woman to cross the Atlantic solo by air (1928); later, while attempting a round-the-world trip in 1937, her plane vanished in the South Pacific. *See:* **Courage**

ECCLESIASTES (book of the Torah [Jewish] and Old Testament Bible [Christian]) (972–932 B.C.) in ancient times ascribed to Solomon, considered part of the Wisdom literature (Wisdom of Solomon) exhorting Jews to seek wisdom; passages on immortality and a history of God's care of the Jews; a philosophical essay, somewhat cynical in tone, opens with the theme that "all is vanity" and continues with passages in praise of wisdom and mercy; current authorities dispute the sole origin of Ecclesiastes to Solomon. *See also* **SOLOMON** *on this list. See:* **Dad, Doctor, Friends, Gossip, Letters, Time**

ECKHART, Meister (Johannes Eckhardt) (1260–1328) German mystical theologian (Roman Catholic, Christian, Dominican Order) entered the order at age 15, studied and taught in the chief schools of his order, notably at Paris, Strasbourg and Cologne and held a series of offices in his order. He wrote scholarly tracts, addressed *The Book of Divine Comfort* to the Queen of Hungary and preached everywhere to the humble and poor, urging them to seek divine spark. Towards the end of his life, he was charged with heresy (unorthodox religious belief) for which he could have been executed by being burned alive if guilty. He was supported by his order, and appealed to Rome, but was denied. The year after he died, Pope John xxii condemned 28 of his propositions as heretical, but from his disciples there sprang up a popular mystical movement in 14th century

Germany, which included many influential religious leaders, some of the Dominican order, who were all intellectual as well as practical preachers and did not separate holiness and learning as the orthodox church did at that time. He was the first writer of speculative prose in German, and from that time German, not Latin, was the language of popular tracts. He stressed the unity of God and the capacity of the individual soul to become one with God during life. *See:* **Depression**

EINSTEIN, Albert, Ph.D. (1879–1955) German Jewish mathematical physicist, was considered learning disabled, dyslexic and a slow learner when a child, but became one of the most respected mathematicians and thinkers who has ever lived; became a naturalized citizen of the USA in 1940 (at age 61); profoundly influenced science in many fields, but is best known for his enunciation of the theory of relativity (1916), science which led to the ability to split the atom and create atomic electrical energy and war-time use (first atomic bombs dropped in 1945 by the USA on Japan which ended World War II); contributed to development of theories of quantum mechanics; also distinguished for his work for peace and justice. *See:* **Adversity, Imagination, Life**

ELIOT, George, pen name of (Mary Anne Evans) (1819–1880) English Victorian poet, romantic writer, journalist who took a man's name for her pseudonym, to create credibility which would have been denied her if it were known a woman was writing her early works; known as a very free, unorthodox thinker; lived in Warwickshire and London from 1854 to 1878 with George Henry Lewes, editor of the *Leader*, who was a married man (an unthinkable breach of convention in that era); among her many novels was *Silas Mariner* (1861) and she wrote 2 books of verse, *The Spanish Gipsy* (1868) and *The Legend of Jubal and Other Poems* (1876); in 1880, she married but died the same year. *See:* **Love, Soul**

EMERSON, Ralph Waldo (1803–1882) American (USA) philosopher, essayist/writer, poet, school-teacher, Unitarian ordained minister, lecturer; born in Boston, attended Harvard; married in 1829, but his wife died of consumption in 1931, at which time he went to Europe; returned to America and remarried in 1835; his philosophy was known as Transcendentalism; stressed intellectual freedom, integrity, self-reliance and realism; the best known of his essays (1841, 1844) are *Self Reliance, Compensation* and *The Over-Soul.* Other volumes are *English Traits* (1856) and *The Conduct of Life* (1860). He is buried in Sleep Hollow Cemetery, Concord, Massachusetts. *See:* **Critics, Friends, Talking, Winners**

EPICTETUS (or Epictitus) (55–136 A.D.) Greek philosopher/teacher, born and for half his life a slave, and permanently crippled young in life; he spent his entire career teaching logic and ethics and promoting a daily regime of Stoic rigorous mental self-examination. He eventually gained his freedom from slavery but was exiled from Rome in 89 (age 45). He held that all individuals (including slaves) are perfectly free to control their own lives and to live in harmony with nature. He argued that we can never fail to be happy if we learn to desire that things should be exactly as they are. *See:* **Desire, Listening**

FEATHER, William (1889–1991) American (USA) philosopher, author, much quoted adages; wrote *As We Were Saying*, wrote and published *The William Feather Magazine; See:* **Life**

FLORIO, John (1553–1626) English author, biographer, teacher, civil servant and lexicographer (person who compiles dictionaries); born in London of Italian parentage; educated at Oxford University; served in several capacities at the court of King James I; wrote works on Italian grammar; compiled an Italian-English dictionary; especially famous for translation of *The Essays of Montaigne* (1603). *See:* **Adversity, Night, Writing**

FOGELBERG, Dan (David Grayling Fogelberg) (1951–?) American (USA) composer, lyricist, touring entertainer, son of a high-school and university music teacher and bandleader and a classically trained pianist, learned piano first, taught himself to play Hawaiian slide guitar; began composing lyrics and music in his teens, and organized two bands; also involved in art and theatre, raised in Illinois; played in coffee houses from his teens onward; left university (arts) after only two years as his popularity grew; spent his later adult life in Colorado (after 1975) (skis); summers in Maine (sailing a 32-foot wooden yawl); released his first music album (of 21) in 1973; first musical hit in 1974; best remembered for *Rivers of Soul, My Old Kentucky Home* and *Run for the Roses* (the Kentucky Derby). *See:* **Chance**

FRANKLIN, Benjamin (1706–1790) American (USA) statesman, scientist and writer, printer, philosopher; born in Boston; went to Philadelphia as a printer in 1723, his common-sense philosophy and wit won attention, especially in *Poor Richard;s Almanack*, published 1732 to 175 and his own auto-biography; helped establish present University of Pennsylvania; disillusioned with British rule in America, he helped to draft and signed American *Declaration of Independence* (1796); was Ambassador to France (1776–1785), took part in the peace negotiations (Britain-USA) (1781–83) at the end of the American Revolutionary War; was popular and trusted in both Britain and America; gained worldwide recognition for his scientific work; experimented with a kite in a thunderstorm and proved identify of lightning and electricity, and for his numerous inventions, which included the lightning rod. *See:* **New Moments**

FRANKHAUSER, Jerry *See:* **Affirmations**

FROMM, Erich, Ph.D., M.D. (1900–1980) German (naturalized USA American) psychoanalyst, professor, writer, who maintained that human needs should be fulfilled by society because the personality is shaped by culture, taught at various universities including New York University during the 1960s; his works include *Man for Himself* (1947), *Psychoanalysis and Religion* (1950), *The Sane Society* (1955), *The Art of Loving* (1956) and *The Anatomy of Human Destructiveness* (1973). *See:* **Practice**

FULLER, Thomas (1608–1661) English clergyman, antiquarian and wit; wrote the collection of short biographies called *The History of the Worthies of England* (1661) known as *Fuller's Worthies. See:* **Anger, Dawn, Depression, Knowledge**

FULGHUM, Robert (1937–?) American (USA) Unitarian clergyman and teacher of drawing, painting and philosophy in Seattle, Washington (both for 32 years); also painter and sculptor; journalist (syndicated newspaper column); motivational speakerl spent early years in Waco, Texas (as a ditch-digger, ranch hand and singing cowboy); sings and plays guitar and mando-cello; founder of an author's rock-and-roll band; published seven best-selling books, including *All I Need to Know I Learned in Kindergarten;* and *Words I*

Wish I Wrote; currently 16 million copies of his books in print, published in 27 languages in 103 countries. *See:* **Life**

GANDHI, Mahatma (Mohandas Karamchand Gandhi) (often called Mahatma, meaning "Great Soul") (1869–1948) Indian statesman, politician, nationalist, pacifist, leader of reform within Hinduism; trained as a lawyer, he went to South Africa and fought for legal rights for Indians (1893); returning to India (1915), he joined the campaign for independence (from Great Britain), leading acts of civil disobedience for which he was frequently jailed; President (1924) Indian National Congress; participated (1931–1946) in the independence negotiations and was regarded as the architect of India's state independence; remembered for his advocacy for nonviolent nonco-operation, his use of hunger strikes, his opposition to Indian caste barriers, in particular his championship of the untouchables (caste) and his work for unity between Hindus, Moslems and Sikhs. **See: Sin**

GAWAIN, Shakti (Contemporary 1955±–?) American (USA) New Age and Yoga Movement motivational author, teacher, educator, retreat leader, publisher, producer of audio tapes, TV talk-show guest; brought up an only child in an academic environment, her parents were atheists; she studied psychology but still sought answers; traveled to India pioneer in the New Age and Yoga Movements, in the field of personal growth and consciousness; adopted the name Hindu name "Shakti" which is the female aspect of the God Shiva and means teacher; believes that nothing is predestined, that everything is a creative process, through visualization, expectation and focus; her many (over 30) books have sold more than 6 million copies in 30 languages, and include *Creative Visualization, Living in the Light, Path of Transformation, Developing Intuition* and *Creating True Prosperity;* founded Nataraj Publishing Company, a Division of New World Library (1998) which publishes all her materials; currently currently lives with her husband in in Marin County, California and Kauai, Hawaii. *See:* **Affirmations, Intuition, Oneself, Risks, Soul**

GAY, John (1865–1732) English poet, playwright, journalist, political critic and satirist; born in Devon, youngest son of his family; lost his parents at an early age and was educated by an uncle; worked as an apprentice to a silk merchant, a steward, and then as secretary to Lord Clarendon, envoy to Hanover (Germany), in his later years lived with two of his patrons, the Duke and Duchess of Queensbury in Wiltshure; in 1732 returned to London, where he is buried in Westminster Abbey; his epitaph reads: "Life is a jest, and all things show it; I thought so once, and now I know it;" of his large and varied body of work, his most famous is the lyrical drama *The Beggar's Opera* (1728) (still performed with original songs for the play) which was the also the basis for *The Three-penny Opera* by Kurt Weil and Bertold Brechti (1928); also wrote sequel *Polly* (1729); wrote libretto for the composer Handelhis literary success enabled him to spend money on gambling and drinking. *See:* **Love**

GENESIS (14th or 13th century B.C.) (Greek means "Origin") First Book of Five Books of Law of the Torah (Jewish text) and Old Testament Bible (Christian), ascribed by tradition to Moses (earliest greatest leader of the Israelite people who led them out of Egypt) most importantly known for telling the story of God's creation of the earth and its people, man's fall from grace (Adam eating the apple in Eden), the great flood (Noah and the ark), traces the history of the great religious patriarchs: Noah, Abraham, Isaac and Jacob, who later became Israel; book ends with the story of Joseph and the migration of Jacob's family to Egypt; the book is generally thought to have been compiled after the Exile, from three main sources of the 9th to 6th centuries B.C.; of critical importance to Jewish and Christian thought. *See:* **Noah, Mispah**

GEORGE, HENRY (1839–1897) American (USA) economist and writer, his book *Progress and Poverty* (1879) advocated a single tax based on unearned income; his views influenced the later formation of the Fabian Party (a British socialist party, founded 1883–84 to promote socialism by gradual reforms, were influential in setting up, in 1900, the Labour Party, early members included George Bernard Shaw and H.G. Wells). *See:* **Success**

GIBRAN, the Prophet (Kahlil Gibran) (1883–1931) Lebanese writer and poet, philosopher, artist, writer; romantic; Arabic (spent last 20 years of his life in the USA writing in English); considered the genius of his age by Arabic-speaking peoples; drawings, paintings

exhibited world-wide; author of 11 books; often illustrated with his own mystical draw-
ings, including his most famous, *The Prophet, The Garden of the Prophet and Prose Poems*; trans-
lated from Lebanese into languages around the world. *See:* **Brothers, Change, Children,
Contradiction, Friends, Gifts, Knowledge, Writing**

GLADSTONE, William (William Ewart Gladstone) (1809–1898) British (English)
theologian, scholar, orator, statesman, politician, Prime Minister (1868–74, 1880–85,
1886 and 1892–94); first entered Parliament under Queen Victoria in 1832 as a Tory
(Conservative); served as Colonial Secretary (1845–6), chancellor of the exchequer
(1852–55 and 1859–1865), reduced income tax and many tariffs; led newly formed Liberal
party to victory in 1868 over Benjamin Disraeli, his life-long political rival; during his
leadership his party disestablished the Irish Church (1869), created a Land Act to pro-
tect Irish tenants (1870), introduced the secret ballot (1872) and carried out many mil-
itary, educational and civil reforms; but he tried unsuccessfully to pass a Home Rule Bill
for Ireland; was never as popular or accepted by Queen Victoria as his rival, Disraeli.
See: **Selfishness**

GOETHE, Johann Wolfgang von (1749–1832) German poet, dramatist and novelist;
for his understanding of literature, art, science and philosophy he was considered one
of the last "renaissance men" (or master of all known knowledge); (contemporary of
Napoleon); considered an easy, natural and personally lyrical writer (unlike his more
precise German predecessors); remembered most for one of his many plays *Faust*
(1808–1832) and his novels *The Sorrows of Werther* (1774) and the *Wilhelm Meister series*
(1796–1829); held posts at the court of the Weimar (duchy, preceding formation of Ger-
many), including Director of the Theater (1791–1817); helped with Schiller and others
to develop the classical German ideal of culture as a process of personal spiritual devel-
opment. *See:* **Home, Honesty, Life**

GOLDSMITH, Oliver (1728–1774) Irish poet and man of letters; poems include *The
Traveller* (1764) and *The Deserted Village* (1770); also wrote *The Vicar of Wakefield* (1766) and a
comedy *She Stoops to Conquer* (1773) which is still performed on stage. **See: Quitting**

GRAYSON, David, pseudonym of (Ray Stannard Baker) (1870–1946) American (USA) author, hard-hitting journalist in Chicago, he also wrote gentle essays under the pseudonym David Grayson, such as *Adventures in Contentment* (1907); was an intimate friend of USA President Wilson, he went to Europe (1918) as his special agent; wrote *Woodrow Wilson and World Settlement* (3 volumes, 1922), edited President Wilson's papers and wrote a biography. *See:* **Doctor**

HAGS, BROOKS *See:* **Mothers-In-Law, Success**

HARPER, The Song of (2650–2600 B.C.) *See:* **Death**

HAWKEN, Paul, Dr. (Contemporary 1940±–?) American (USA) author, entrepreneur, environmentalist, educator, lecturer, seminar leader, journalist; futurist, founded Erewhon Trading Company, a natural foods wholesaling business in the 1960 and was an important figure in the natural food movement in the 1970s; founded Smith & Hawken mail order garden supply company in 1979; in 1987 wrote *Growing a Business* which became a successful Public Broadcasting System show of the same title; a pioneer in the natural foods movement, and environmentally and ecologically sound business practices ethics development, he has become one of the leading proponents with respect to ecological practices for businesses, environmental sustainability and the restorative economy; winner of many diverse awards and at least 4 honorary doctorates, he is author of dozens of articles, scientific papers and six books which have been published in over 50 countries in 28 languages, including: *Seven Tomorrows* (1980), *The Next Economy* (1983), *The Ecology of Commerce* (1993) which is the number 1 text on business and the environment in 67 business schools, *Factor Ten—The Next Industrial Revolution* (1999). *See:* **Money**

HAZLETT, William (1778–1830) English essayist, literary and dramatic critic, works include *Characters in Shakespeare's Plays* (1817), *Lectures on the English Poets* (1818), *Lectures on the English Comic Writers* (1819), *Table Talk* (1821–22) and *The Spirit of the Age* (1825). With Samuel Coleridge, he led in interpreting Shakespeare and Elizabethan drama; his perceptive essays such as *Going on a Journey* and *My First Acquaintance with Poets* are notable for their clear, easy to understand style. *See:* **Personality, Self-Worth**

HENLEY, W.E. (William Ernest Henley) (1849–1903) English poet, author, critic, play-write, and editor of the *Magazine of Art* (1882–1886), the *National Observer;* had suffered tuberculosis as a child, including 20 months in a hospital and amputation of one of his legs; as an adult friend of writer, Robert Louis Stevenson, he was said to have been the inspiration of the pirate character *Long John Silver* in Stevenson's *Treasure Island;* he collaborated with Stevenson on four plays (1880–1885) and was also a joint compiler of a seven-volume dictionary of slang (1894–1904); his own works included many poetry collections including *Collected Poems* (1878) and his best-known poem *Invictus* (1875) which ends: "It matters not how strait the gate, How charged with punishment the scroll, I am the master of my fate; I am the captain of my soul." *See:* **Fate**

HERBERT, George (1593–1633) English author (Latin and English), metaphysical poet; Anglican priest and preacher, born of a noble family, brother of Baron Herbert of Chirbury; one of 10 children whose father died when he was 3 years of age; his mother was patron to John Donne; graduate of Cambridge University; first 2 poems published in Latin in 1612 (19 years of age); was appointed Public Orator and Reader in Rhetoric at Cambridge (1620–1628) which required him to orate in Latin the sentiments of the university on public occasions; refused prestigious public office appointment to become an Anglican priest (1930); none of his work was published during his lifetime; died of consumption in 1633; but his work was published by his friend posthumously, *The Temple* (1633) and *Easter Wings* (1633). His poetry combined a homely familiarity with religious experience, and was notable for quietness of tone, precision of language, intelligent reverence and fanciful conceits (witty thoughts or expressions, often far-fetched). *See:* **Death**

HERICILITUS (5th century B.C.) Greek philosopher, Ionian; critic of Xenophanes and Pythagorus; "Much information does not teach wisdom…" he said, and "The universe is perpetual motion, nothing but conflict and strife; experience is illusion," therefore "if everything we interact with is constantly changing, we cannot learn anything lasting about it, because it is constantly changing and becoming something else, thus meaning scientific (static) knowledge is impossible." *See:* **Character, Shame**

HILLEL (70 B.C.–A.D. 10 or 40+) Jewish rabbi, founder of a religious school (Hillel Bet) which continued for 400 years: born in Babylonia (an ancient kingdom on the Tigris and Euphates Rivers, in southern Mesopatamia, present day Iraq), descendant of the family of David; his history part of the Talmud (Jewish historical records) although born poor, he studied religious law all his life; at the age of 40, went to Jerusalem (presently in Israel), the center of Jewish religion, where during the next 40 years he was said to have worked as a day-laborer, continued to study religion and was said to have learned all languages; at age 80 became the spiritual head of the Israeli people for the next 40 years (to 120 years of age), one of his teachings being: "Do not unto others what is hateful to thee;" lived at approximately the same time period as Jesus Christ (Christian) *See:* **Now Moments**

HINDUISM (4000 B.C. to 2200 B.C.) generally regarded as the world's oldest organized religion, Hinduism differs from western religions in that it does have one single founder, a specific theological system, a single system of morality or a central religious organization; it consists of thousands of different religious groups that have evolved in India since 1500 B.C. and is now the third largest religion, claiming about 800 million followers worldwide; tolerates the existence of multiple gods and goddesses; contains many sects, each dedicated to a particular deity (god); most important texts are *Vedas*, the *Upanishadas*; the *Mahabhaarata*; followers believe in transfer of one soul after death into another body, a continuing cycle of birth, life, death and rebirth through many lifetimes; Karma (destiny) determines how you will live your next life and into which caste you will be born; good works can improve your chances of being born into a higher caste, evil will increase your chances of being in a lower caste; meditation is often practiced, with Yoga being most common; Hinduism has a reputation for being tolerant of other religions; a common saying being: "The truth is One, but different sages call it by Different Names"; was based on a a vertical caste system with 5 castes (the bottom being untouchables, or outcasts) existed for nearly 2,000 years and was formally abolished only in 1949 but in general practice, still remains a significant force throughout India; the caste into which one was born determining whom you may marry, work with, even drink eat or talk to. *See:* **Glory**

HINELUS *See:* **Shame**

HIPPOCRATES (460–377 B.C.) Greek physician who is considered the father of medicine; attempting to put medicine on a scientific basis, he stressed the importance of clinical study, rational observation of the body and its functions and ethical treatment of patients; present day doctors take an oath of honor and ethics called the Hippocratic Oath inspired by his teachings, and in his honor, upon graduation from their medical studies. *See:* **Doctor, Healing**

HITOPAEDESA (5th century) Indian, composed by a Brahman (Hindu teacher who believes that all creation is one unity); means "good advice" and is a collection of ethical tales and fables compiled from the older work called Pancha-tantra (five books) which was compiled to teach the sons of a king; has reappeared in many languages both in the East and the West and is considered the source of many familiar and widely known stories; ultimately became familiar in Europe as *Pilpay's Fables*; stories are popular through Hindustan; there are various editions of the text and several translations. *See:* **Separation**

HOLLAND, Josiah G. (1819–1881) American (USA) journalist, writer, editor, owner of *Scribner's Monthly:The Century Magazine*, wrote many magazine articles, the book, *The Life of Abraham Lincoln*, his writing style considered readily read by commonplace readers rather than the more stilted and scholarly writing common in his time. *See:* **Work**

HOLT, John (John Caldwell Holt) (1923–1985) American (USA); anti-nuclear war activist, teacher, author; creator of concept and and one of the best known proponents of home schooling, book-store owner, publisher of the first home schooling magazine, *Growing Without Schooling*; after graduating university joined the U.S. Navy and served in the Pacific during World War II; believed that nuclear war was the world's greatest danger; started in the mailroom and became executive director of the New York branch of the United World Federalists in 6 years, but left the organization in 1952; became a teacher in Colorado, then Boston; well known for his first two books *How Children Fail* and *How Children Learn*, detailing his philosophy of education; believed that fear of various kinds precluded children learning in the public system; became an advocate of home schooling; believed that children would learn naturally if given the freedom to follow their own interests and given a rich assortment of resources; a line of thought which became known as "unschooling." *See:* **Action**

HOLMES, Oliver Wendell (1809–1894) American (USA) physician, poet, writer and essayist; born Cambridge, Massachusetts, graduate of Harvard University; his witty, polished essays and many of his poems are contained in *Poems* (1836); his sketches and contributions to magazines in *The Autocrat of the Breakfast Table* (1858); *The Professor at the Breakfast Table* (1860) and *The Poet at the Breakfast Table* (1872); his verse provided poems and good humor for average Americans, *Old Ironsides, The Chambered Nautilus, The Deacon's Masterpiece, The Wonderful One-Hoss Shay;* he also wrote medical pamphlets of considerable importance; his several novels were less successful, but have recently been appreciated as the first American psychological novels. *See:* **Direction**

HOPPER, Edward (1882–1967) American (USA) painter whose works depict the realism of American life, excels in sunlit streets and house, especially in New York and New England (upper north-east USA); his famous paintings include *House by the Railroad* (1925), *From Williamsburg Bridge* (1928), *Sunday Morning* (1930), *Gas* (1940) and *Nighthawks* (1942). *See:* **Imagination**

HORACE (Quintus Horatius Flaccus) (65–8 B.C.) Italian (Roman) soldier, poet and writer of odes; he fought with Brutus at Phillipi (42 B.C.) but was introduced to Maecenas's circle (38 B.C.) and became a loyal supporter and friend of Augustus; his books of *Odes* deal with a wide variety of subjects, imitating earlier poets; the *Satires* and *Epistles* discuss literary, political and moral themes and literary criticism. *See:* **Beginnings**

HOUSTON, Jean, Ph.D.? (1941–?) American (USA) (claims dual doctorates in philosophy of religion from Columbia-Union Theological Seminary and psychology at Union Graduate School but these are disputed by both institutions) psychologist, scholar, mythologist, scientist, teacher, educator, theologian, writer, motivational speaker; seminar leader, actress and director of Broadway stage plays; born the daughter of a comedy writer for Bob Hope, her mother a Christian Scientist; her family moved constantly as a child and by age 12, she had attended 29 schools, including a Roman Catholic school; attended New York's High School for the Performing Arts, Barnard College; traveled to Greece at age 19 to pursue interests in archaeology and ancient religions; married to Robert Masters, a psychotherapist who co-authored the Masters-Johnson report on sexual behavior; was involved in drugs, LSD and others, with her husband; became involved in Occultism and Parapsychology; promoted seminars at the Foundation for Mind Research, teaches meditation and self-hypnosis; author many books including *The Possible Human;* believes in communication with the dead and the influence of the dead on living persons, including (now) controversial counseling/teaching of (now) Senator Hilary Clinton, wife of former President of the U.S., Bill Clinton, whom she believes is the current embodiment of Eleanor Roosevelt. *See:* **Laughter**

HUBBARD, Elbert, M.A., LL.B. (Honorary) (1856–1915) American (USA) school-teacher, freelance newspaperman, printer, editor, publisher, essayist, writer, lecturer, head of sales for a manufacturing company, entrepreneur; born the son of a farmer/country doctor; his own education given as "University of Hard Knocks," Honorary M.A. (Tufts University) and LL.B. (law) (Chicago) (USA); founded Roycroft Press at East Aurora, New York in 1892 (age 36) which continues today as Roycrofters Corporation (employing 800 people), wrote "about 10,000 magazine articles," many books including *One Day; No Enemy But Himself: Little Journeys; Time and Chance; Life of John Brown; A Message to Garcia; etc.* His hobbies were horseback riding, swimming, rowing and care of flowers and gardening; died with his wife in the Irish Sea when the U.S. *Lusitainia* was sunk by a German submarine in 1917 (during World War I). *See:* **Failure, Life**

HUGO, Victor (1802–1885) (Victor Marie Hugo) French poet, novelist, dramatist; in his plays, broke through classical restrictions; in his poems he invented or restored innumerable styles in meter and harmony; also wrote epic and satirical poetry; considered a prolific genius who profoundly enriched French poetry and opened the way for much modern stylistic changes; as a novelist, notably in *Notre Dame de Paris* (1831) and *Les Miserables* (1862), he influenced romantic fiction throughout Europe. *See:* **Ideas**

HUNEKER, James Gibbons (1860–1921) American (USA) essayist, critic of music, art and drama. *See:* **Art**

HUNT, Leigh (James Henry Leigh Hunt) (1784–1859) English poet, essayist, lyricist, critic and editor; edited weeklies *Examiner* and *Liberal*; contributed to many others; a friend of contemporary writers, he strongly influenced Shelley and Keats; some lyrics such as *Abhou Ben Adhem* and *Jenny Kissed Me*, essays and his *Autobiography* (1850) are still much read. *See:* **Emotions**

HUXLEY, Thomas (1825–95) British (English) biologist, scientist and writer; while serving as marine surgeon aboard H.M.S. *Rattlesnake*, he collected marine specimens from the Pacific Ocean; a leading proponent of Darwin's Theory on the Origin of Special (or Evolution) by Natural Selection (1859), he wrote himself on evolution, anatomy, physiology and other fields of science; his books include *Zoological Evidences of Man's Place in Nature* (1863) and *Science and Culture* (1881). *See:* **Success**

INDIAN (NORTH AMERICAN) SAYING, OLD See: **Life**

ISAIAH (late 8th century B.C.) a Major Prophet of the Torah (Jewish) or Old Testament Bible (Christian), the book attributed to him considered by many scholars to be the work of at least three authors; Chapters 1 to 25 are metrical prophecies, directed chiefly against Syria and Assyria; Chapters 26 to 39 form a section of prophetic prose narrative; Chapters 40 to 46 are metrical prophecies on the theme of redemption; many passages in the book are taken by Christians to refer directly to Christ. *See:* **Suffering**

JAMES, Gospel (or Epistle, Letter) (Saint James) to Roman Catholics (Christian) (40? B.C.–30 A.D.?) book of the New Testament (Christian), written by Saint James, one of the 12 Apostles (disciples) of Christ; called James the Less, son of Alphaeus (see books of Mark, Matthew and Acts) believed to be a kinsman of Jesus Christ and head of the church in Jerusalem; feast day May 1st; *See:* **Life**

JAMES, Henry (1843–1916) American (USA) one of the most celebrated of American novelists, short story writer, dramatist, travel writer, literary critic, auto-biographer, while studying law at Harvard University, decided to switch to literature; he became a naturalized British subject in 1915 as a political statement about World War I (1914–18); spent most of his adult life in Europe; a recurrent theme in his fiction is the contrast between ingenuous, through often charming, Americans and the cultured, sophisticated Europeans and between the raw American Scene and the centuries-laden, rich civiliza-tion of Europe, all on a level of wealth and social position. Among his many novels are *A Passionate Pilgrim, and Other Tales* (1881), *Daisy Miller* (1879), *Washington Square* (1881), *The Portrait of a Lady* 1881), *The Bostonians* (1886), *The Awkward Age* (1899), *The Wings of the Dove* (1902), *The Ambassadors* (1903) and *The Golden Bowl* (1904). Among his short stories, *The Turn of the Screw* is perhaps most familiar. His drams were largely unsuccessful on stage, his literary criticism has had much influence on American writers, his autobiographical works include *A Small Boy and Others* (1913). His prefaces to his own novels are consid-ered important critical pieces. *See:* **Home**

JEREMIAH (late 6th and early 7th century B.C.) a major prophet and teacher and book of Torah (Jewish) or Old Testament Bible (for Christians), lived at the time of the col-lapse of Assyria and the fall of Jerusalem; urged moral reform, emphasizing an individ-ual relationship between God and man; which marked a transition from the idea of an exclusive national (Hebrew) relationship between God and only the Jews; had a profound influence on New Testament Christian teaching relating to his life and prophecies. *See:* **Dad, Death, Spots**

JERROLD, Douglas (1803–1857) English, writer, satirist, political commentator, dramatist, play writer and producer, printer, compositor, sailor; born the son of an actor, joined the navy at the age of 10, but was deeply upset by the way the officers treated the men on board ship, in particular the floggings for minor offences, and it gave him a lifelong hatred of authority; at 12 became a printers apprentice, then a compositor on the *Sunday Monitor,* rose to become the newspaper's drama critic, wrote plays including *Fifteen Years of a Drunkard's Life* (1828), *Black-Eyed Susan* (1829), and *The Prisoner of Ludgate* (1831). In 1831, started the journal *Punch* in London, which failed after 17 issues. Later, he joined forces with others to form *Punch Magazine,* which combined satirical humor and political comment., which he wrote for over a period of 16 years. Writing under the pen name Q, he wrote several powerful political attacks on inequality in 19th century Britain, which gained the magazine the reputation as a radical journal. Charles Dickens was his friend and described Jerrold's book, *The Story of a Feather* as "a beautiful book." He worked on and for numerous magazines and journals including *Lloyd's Weekly Newspapers* (1852–57) *See:* **Happiness**

JEWISH THEOLOGICAL SEMINAR *See: Life*

JOHN, Gospel (or Epistle, letters) (Saint James) to Roman Catholics (Christian) (40±? B.C.–50± A.D.) author of Book of John (New Testament Christian) contemporary, friend, disciple, writer, and one of the 12 Apostles of Jesus Christ who knew Christ during his lifetime, author of the Fourth Gospel (book) of the Christian New Testament; the three Epistles of John and the book, Revelation (all parts of the New Testament) have also been attributed to him; brother was Saint James, known as James the Greater, also a disciple of Jesus Christ (Symbol a young man; Feast Day December 27th. *See:* **Sin**

JOHNSON, Samuel (1709–1784) English author, poet, critic, essayist, moralist and lexicographer; his first major work was in satiric verse, *London* (1738) and *The Vanity of Human Wishes* (1749). His *Rambler* essays appeared 1750-52. Despite extreme difficulties, he published in 1755 *Dictionary of the English Language* which won him immediate fame, tended to stabilize the English usage (spelling and word usage) for the first time; his 1765 edition of Shakespeare with preface and notations is still highly respected; many further essays and books followed; he was considered the dictator of literary taste in London, and because of his literary judgment and his integrity, he became the dominant literary figure of his age. *See:* **Early Riser, Honesty, Perseverance**

JONES, F.P. (1950±–?) contemporary American (USA) author. *See:* **Death**

JUNG, Carl Gustav, M.D. (1885–1961) Swiss psychiatrist, writer, teacher, in 1912 founded school of analytical psychology; as first President of the International Psychoanalytic Association, he was second only to Sigmund Freud in the movement; they worked together until differences of approach caused a formal break (1913); Jung conceived of libido as primal, nonsexual energy and postulated two systems in the unconscious: the personal (repressed events of personal life) and the collective unconscious (racial archetypes of inherited tendencies, such as the hero and the mother goddess); introduced the terms "introversion" and "extraversion," writings include *The Psychology of the Unconscious* (1916). *See:* **Aspirations, Creativity, Personality**

KABBALA (The) (100 to 1000 B.C.) (also referred to as Cabala, Quaballah, Kabalah or Kabbalah, etc.) ancient books of Jewish mystical thought which form the sacred written and oral tradition and history of the Jewish people; the word derives from the root "to receive, to accept" and in many cases is used synonymously with "tradition"; according to Jewish tradition, the *Torah* (= "Law," the first 5 books of the Old Testament Bible for Christians) was created prior to the world and was advice to God on such matters as the creation of human kind; when Moses received the written law from God (the 10 Commandments), tradition has it that he also received the oral law, which was not written down but passed from generation to generation; at times the oral law has been referred to as "Kabbbalah" or the oral tradition; believed by Jews to be divine and understandable by diligent study of the text; the Kaballah, studied and commented upon down through the ages, is still an important component of Jewish theological training and study. *See:* **Love, Tears**

KEATS, John (1795–1821) English poet, writer; wrote *Endymion* (1818), his famous Odes the famous *Ode to a Nightingale; Ode to a Grecian Urn; Ode on Melancholy; Ode to Psyche; Ode to Autumn;* and *Hyperion* (1820); his letters are considered among the finest sensual poetry in the English language, he died of tuberculosis at age 25. *See:* **Truth**

KEMPIS, Thomas à (1379–1471) German monk (Augustinian Order, Roman Catholicism, Christian), author of devotional works; he is generally supposed to have written *The Imitation (or Following) of Christ*; lived most of his life in the convent of Mount St. Agnes near Zwolle (Netherlands). *See:* **Criticism**

KENNEDY, Ethel (1890?–1990?); American (USA) mother and homemaker; wife of Joseph Patrick Kennedy, real estate and cinema financier, Ambassador to Great Britain (1937); parents of 12 children, among them John Fitzgerald Kennedy (1917–1963) 35th President of the USA (assassinated in Dallas, Texas), Robert Francis Kennedy (1925–1968) (presidential candidate, assassinated) and Senator Edward (Ted) M. Kennedy (1932–?). *See:* **Heart**

KENNEDY, Edward ("Teddy") M. (Edward Moore Kennedy) (1932–?) American (USA) United States Senator, elected in 1962 from the state of Massachusetts to fill the vacancy left by his older brothers, assassinated President John F. Kennedy and also assassinated Presidential aspirant, Robert F. Kennedy; son of Joseph F. Kennedy, industrialist and USA Ambassador to England; a Democrat, he has been re-elected to the seat ever since (41 years); despite a back injury, intermittent problems with alcohol control and a controversial accident (1969) in which he drove his car off a bridge and a woman passenger was drowned, he has remained influential in the Senate and national politics; considered a liberal, he ran in the 1980 Presidential nomination but lost to (later President) Jimmy Carter. *See:* **Time**

KHAN, Hazrat Inayat *See:* **Words**

KHAYAM, Omar (The Rubiyat of) (1044–1123) Iranian (Persian); poet, mathematician, astronomer, scientist, historian, mystic, sage; "Khamam" means tent-maker; it was common for Iranian poets to take their name from their occupation; he was Omar, the son of Abraham, the tentmaker; "Rubiyat" means book; as his father was before him, he was briefly in the trade of tent-making, but was favored by the king (Sultan) Malik Shah for whom he reformed the Muslim calendar; soon, however, he rejected the court life in favor of scientific studies and literary pursuits; his scientific contributions were multiple and complex, including in the fields of geometry, algebra, mathematics, binomial theorem, equations, measuring specific gravity and metaphysics; in the west, he is most famous for his more than 100 quatrain poems (four-line stanzas) extra-ordinary for their love passion and beauty of imagery, which were translated first into English by Edward FitzGerald, an English poet and translator who lived 1809–1883; although the translation gained popularity slowly in the west, it has ultimately became the most loved collection of poems in the English language. *See:* **Now Moments**

KIPLING, Rudyard (1865–1936) English author, journalist; poet; his early writings were based on the life of the English, civilian and military, in India, where he worked on a newspaper; on his return to England (1889) he became a successful author of poems, short stories and novels; following the publication of *Plain Tails from the Hills* (1888). His other prose books include the well-known *The Jungle Book* (1894), *Second Jungle Book* (1895) as well as *Stalky and Co.* (1899), *Kim* (1901) and *Just So Stories* (1902); his interests were in the field of men using their power and skills, as representing the self-sacrificing administrator upholding civilization; considered a great story teller; his style is intensely vivid and concrete; collected poems include: *Barrack Room Ballads* (1892) and *Recessional and Other Poems* (1899). *See:* **Addiction**

KLESSER, Grenville *See:* **Good**

KOESTENBAUM, Peter, Ph.D. (1921–?) philosopher, professor, leadership trainer, lecturer, orator, writer, musician, scientist; educated at Stanford University (physics and philosophy), B.A.; at Harvard (philosophy) M.A.; Boston University (philosophy) Ph.D., also attending University of California (Berkeley) in music and philosophy; taught in the Philosophy Department of San Jose State University (California) for 34 years; for 25 years has worked with psychologists and psychiatrists in seminars, lectures and books exploring the relationship between psychiatry and the healing potential of philosophy; founder and Chairman of PIB and the Koestenbaum Institute headquartered in Stockholm, Sweden and Los Angeles, California; has lectured in 36 countries on five continents; his leadership training/business management/strategic thinking/marketing books (translated into many languages) include: *The Inner Side of Greatness, The Heart of Business, Freedom and Accountability At Work;* his philosophical books include *The Vitality of Death, The New Image of the Person, Managing Anxiety, Choosing to Love* and *Is There an Answer to Death? See:* **Creativity**

KRISHNAMURTI, T. (1895–1985) Contemporary Indian philosopher, author; educated in England and Europe; said to have been found (1909) by an aura about his head denoting him as the reincarnated Lord Krishna, and New Messiah, as widely believed by his followers in the Theosophical Society, treated like royalty wherever he went; but he renounced all claims to Divinity at the age of 34 and went into seclusion; foundations have been created in his name around the world (including Canada), and his large body of written work includes: *The Awakening of Intelligence, Beginnings of Learning, Beyond Violence, The Book of Life, Can Humanity Change?; Commentaries on Living; Education and the Significance of Life; The Ending of Time, Eight Conversations, The First and Last Freedom; See:* **Learning (× 2)**

KUBBLER-ROSS, Elizabeth, Ph.D. (Contemporary 1950±–?) American (USA) psychiatrist, author who researched and wrote about the the subject of "near-death" or "life after death" experiences. *See:* **Soul**

Lao TSU (Old Master) Chinese Taoist, philosopher; *See* **TSU** *in this list. See:* **Self**

LARCOM, Lucy *See:* **Warmth**

LATIN PROVERB, (600 B.C.–1600 A.D.) **Latin** = related to or written in the Latin language; now considered a dead (or ancient, non-active) source language, but still used by Roman Catholic (Christian) church for its rites and masses world-wide; earliest record 600 B.C.; with the rise of the Roman Empire, the language spread world-wide, used commonly throughout Europe until 1600 A.D.; may be a person whose mother language is a Romance language (and who lives in a country where they are spoken) which are a group of languages developed from Latin (includes French, Italian, Provencal, Portuguese, Romanian, Spanish, Catalan, Sardinian, etc.); **Proverb** = a brief familiar maxim of folk wisdom. *See:* **Personality**

LAURIER, Wilfred, Sir (Sir Wilfred Laurier) (1841–1919), Canadian (Roman Catholic Christian) lawyer, orator, editor, soldier, parliamentarian, statesman, Prime Minister of Canada (Liberal); born in St. Lin, Quebec; educated at McGill University; called to the bar (1864); editor *Le Detricheur (1866–67)*, Ensign, Athabaskaville Infantry (1869–1878), first elected Member of Legislative Assembly (1871), Liberal, party leader (1887–1919) first French Canadian and first Roman Catholic Prime Minister of Canada (1896–1910), longest period a Prime Minister has held office in Canadian history; leading statesman, his political record includes: spirited defense of Louis Riel and the Manitoba School problems (1885); attended Queen Victoria's Diamond Jubilee Celebration in London, England as Canada's representative (1897) and was knighted; helped create the Yukon Territory (1898); resolved the Alaska Boundary Dispute (1903); promoted construction of a second transcontinental railway (1903), created provinces of Saskatchewan and Alberta (1905), Naval Service Bill (1910), Leader of the Opposition (1911–1919); as a French Canadian, respected British tradition and authority, but worked to keep Canada united; after serving for 45 years in Parliament, died (1919) and buried in Ottawa; his funeral procession was one of the first public events in Canada to be recorded on film. *See:* **Addiction**

LEVITICUS, the third book of the Torah (Jewish) or Old Testament Bible (Christian) names for the Levites, which contains general liturgical Hebrew religious laws concerning worship, sacrifice and purification and and social laws regarding personal conduct. *See:* **Gossip**

LINCOLN, Abe (known as *Honest Abe*) (Abraham Lincoln) (1809–1865) American (USA); storekeeper, postmaster, surveyor, lawyer, orator, politician; 16th President (Republican) of the USA (1861–1865), statesman, orator, lawyer, a Republican, born in a long cabin in Kentucky and brought up in the backwoods of Indiana, he had almost no formal schooling, but was a devoted student of people and the books he could buy or borrow, taught himself law (1837), practiced law in Springfield, Illinois; elected to Congress (1847); campaigned against slavery; his election as President, on an anti-slavery program, provoked the American Civil War (1861–1865) when the southern states tried to secede from the Union; issued the Proclamation of Emancipation (Freedom from Slavery) (1863); delivered the oft-quoted Gettysburg Address in dedication of a civil war cemetery in which he used the words: "government of the people, by the people, for the people, shall not perish from the earth"; he promised amnesty and moderation to the Secessionist south but five days after General Lee's surrender, he was himself assassinated by John Wilkes Booth, a southern fanatic; *See:* **Future**

LINDBERGH, Anne Morrow, B.A. (Anne Morrow Spenser Lindbergh) American (USA) (1906–2001) writer, philosopher, inspirational writer; aviation pioneer, wife of Charles A. Lindbergh, (pioneer U.S. aviator who made the first solo flight across the Atlantic ocean (1927) flying New York to Paris, 3600 miles in 33½ hours); she was the first licensed woman glider pilot in the United States and she was her husband's co-pilot, navigator and radio operator on various history-making trips and explorations, charting potential air routes for commercial airlines; together. they set a transcontinental speed record from Los Angeles to New York in 14 hours, 45 minutes (1932) when she was 7 months pregnant; she wrote about their various adventures in various books, including *North to the Orient* (1935), and *Listen to the Wind* (1938); other works include *Gift from the Sea* (1955), *Bring Me A Unicorn* (1972), *Hour of Gold, Hour of Lead* (1973) and others; the Lindberghs were victims of one of the first tragic celebrity crimes as their first-born child, Charles Junior, was kidnapped at the age of 20 months and murdered (1932); the kidnapping lead the Congress of the USA to adopt the Lindbergh Act which made kidnapping and transfer of children across state lines illegal as a result of this much-publicized tragedy; the Lindberghs went on to have 5 more children; among other prestigious awards, the National Geographic Society awarded its Hubbard Gold Medal to Anne Lindbergh (1934) for her accomplishments in 40,000 miles of exploratory flying over 5 continents. *See:* **Time**

(The) LION KING (1994) originally a very lavish New York musical play which ran successfully on Broadway for many years, in Toronto in 2000–2004; made into a Disney animated film first in 1994 and re-released and improved in 2003, which tells the story of Simba, a young lion cub, goes through various trials to achieve manhood including fighting and defeating his own treacherous uncle, the evil Scar, to ultimately achieve his role as Lion King; along the way meets and falls in love with a lioness, Nala; music, sets, and spectacular in both the play and the movie variations lush, lavish and luxurious sets, as befits its jungle environment; some memorable songs included: *The Circle of Life* and *Can You Feel the Love Tonight?*. *See:* **Taking**

LOMBARDI, Vince, Coach (Vincent Lombardi) football coach, teacher, businessman, born in Brooklyn, New York, one of 5 children in an Italian immigrant family; raised in the Roman Catholic (Christian) faith and studied for the priesthood for two years before transferring to St. Francis Prepatory School, where he was a star fullback on the football team. Attended New York City's Fordham University on a football scholarship and graduated with a business degree (1937); worked days at a finance company and studied law at night for 2 years; then took a teaching job at a high-school where he taught Latin, algebra, physics and chemistry, and coached the football, basketball and baseball teams. He began coaching for Fordham University (1947) and the United States Military Academy at West Point (1949–1954), which began a long and outstanding coaching career at various Universities. In 1970, he professional coaching records stood at 105-35-6 and the National Football League acclaimed him "1960s Man of the Decade." In 2000, ESPN named him Coach of the Century. He died of intestinal cancer in 1970. *See:* **Winning**

LONG, Cec *See:* **Love**

LONGFELLOW, Henry Wadsworth (1807–1882) American (USA) author, poet, professor; born Portland, Maine; best known for his highly popular poetry and long narrative poems on historical subjects, especially *The Song of Hiawatha* (1855), a sentimental treatment of Indian legends and *Evangeline* (1847) based on the expulsion of the Acadians from Nova Scotia; sentimental and inspirational poetry included *The Courtship of Miles Standish* (1858), *Paul Revere's Last Ride (in Tales of a Wayside Inn* (1865), *Excelsior* and *The Village Blacksmith. See:* **Life, Success**

LOWELL, James Russell (1819–1891) American (USA) romantic poet and editor; his satirical works include *Bigelow Papers* (1848), political and social lampoons written in Yankee dialect; his literary criticism includes *Fireside Travels* (1884); his *Letters of James Russell Lowell* (1893) and *New Letters* (1932) are commentaries on public affairs and the literary activities of his generation *See:* **Honesty**

LUBBOCK, John, Sir (Baron Sir John Lubbock of Avebury) (1834–1913) English banker, statesman and naturalist; as a member of Parliament from 1870, he introduced many reform bills, especially in banking, including legislation establishing bank holidays; his scientific contributions were in entomology (branch of zoology that deals with insects) and anthropology (origin, developments and customs of mankind) and include his *Prehistoric Times* (1865), long used as a textbook in several languages; popular works include *Ants, Bees and Wasps* (1882) and *The Pleasures of Life* (two volumes 1887–89). He was created Baron Avebury in 1900. *See:* **Life**

MANN, Stella Terrill (1913–?) Austrian ballet dancer, teacher, school administrator; started Ballet School in London, England in 1946 and ran the school and later full-time college for 40 years; when accreditation began, hers was one of the first schools to be accredited because of the high standards of all-around dance training; she included Modern and Jazz dance instructions for professional performers; began painting after retirement and exhibits and sells her art in London; plays classical piano and incorporates it into dance music; benefactress of a bursary to encourage young (15 to 17 year old) students in training. *See:* **Life**

MASEFIELD, John (John Edward Masefield) (1878–1967) English, poet, critic and novelist; was poet laureate of England 1930–1967; a boyhood spent at sea was the basis for his first poems *Salt Water Balads* (1902); first long narrative poem *The Everlasting Mercy* (1911) won him fame; later poems best known included *The Widow in the Bye Street* (1912) and *Dauber* (1913); also author of novels, including *Sard Harker* (1924), plays, books and sketches for boys. *See:* **Winning, Wisdom**

MENCKEN, H.L. (Henry Louis Mencken) (1880–1956) American (USA) writer, journalist, book reviewer, political commentator, food book writer, and controversial most prominent critic of American life of his day; part of his voluminous life-time writings, his *Prejudices*, in 6 volumes (1919–1927), a collection of essays and reviews, satirizes organized religion, business and middle-class values; particularly noted was his coverage of the Darwinist precipitated Scopes Trial in Tennessee; his rhetoric was as deadly as a rifle; but he was positively enthusiastic about Twain, Conrad, Brahms, Beethoven and Bach and sea foods available near his native Chesapeake Bay, New England; an able linguistic scholar, he published *The American Language* (1919); *See:* **Man**

MELTON, George (Contemporary 1960±–?) American (USA) Fundamentalist Southern Baptist Christian, member of a number of Bible Quartets including the Claiborne Brothers Quartet, the Gospelaires Quartet of Southern California, the Four Lads Quartet and the Ambassador Quartet (an acappella quartet, voice only, in which he sang tenor); graduate of the Cincinnati Bible Seminary; Melton family songs include: *Makin' a New Start, You're Not Alone, Heavenly Choir and I Can't Walk. See:* **Peace**

MENCIUS (Mandarin Meng-tse) (372–289 B.C.) Chinese sage who believed that man was innately good, not selfish; but man will be free to do good only if he has the peace of mind which follows from material well-being; believed that Rulers must ensure such security or be deposed; *The Book of Mencius* is a classic commentary on the doctrines of Confucius (see Confucius). *See:* **Children**

MICHENER, James (James Albert Michener) (1907–?) American (USA) author; his works include *Tales of the South Pacific* (1947) later made into the musical comedy movie *South Pacific*, *The Fires of Spring* (1949), *Return to Paradise* (1951) and *The Voice of Asia* (1951); best-selling books include *Sayonara* (1954) *Hawaii* (1959), *Centennial* (1974), *Space* (1982) and I*texas* (1985). *See:* **Contentment**

MICHELANGELO (Michelangelo Buonarotti) (1475–1564) Florentine (Italian) painter, sculptor, architect and poet; a towering unmatched figure of the Renaissance art world; raised in Florence but went to Rome on the death of his patron where he carved the *Pieta* of St. Peter's Cathedral, which immediately made him famous; then went back to Florence where he carved the magnificent *David*; in 1505 the Pope Julius II called him back to Rome to work on his tomb, a work which occupied him for the next 40 years; the *Moses* of Pietro (1513–16) is part of this work and one of his most famous carvings; Julius II also commissioned him to paint, in Rome, the ceiling of the Sistine Chapel (the private chapel of the Pope) (completed 1512); its subject, from Genesis, is the creation of the world, the Fall and man's continuance in sin; he worked on the Medici chapel in Florence for 14 years (1520–34); in 1534, he began painting *The Last Supper* behind the High Altar in the Sistine Chapel (25 years after the ceiling, completed in 1541); most of these works remain largely intact in Italy today. *See:* **Aging**

MILLAY, Edna St. Vincent (1892–1950) American (USA) lyric poet, first attracted notice with *Renascence* (1912) and later gained a wide audience with her volumes: *A Few Figs from Thistles* (1920), *Second April* (1921) and *The Ballad of the Harp-Weaver* (1922); also wrote dramatic verse and librettos for opera and radio; her sonnets, in various volumes, are much admired. *See:* **Abundance, Action, Candles**

MILLE, Agnes de, *See:* **de Mille, Agnes,** *in this list. See:* **Silence**

MILLER, Henry (1891–1980) American (USA) author; best known for his novels *Tropic of Cancer* (1934) and *Tropic of Capricorn* (1937) **See: Immortality**

MILLS, K.G., Ph.D. (Honorary) (Contemporary 1940±–?) (Kenneth George Mills) Canadian, concert pianist, conductor, composer, poet, writer, teacher, lecturer, metaphysics philosopher, painter (acrylic), born St. Stephen, New Brunswick, studied piano privately in Toronto, Aspen, Colorado and New York; debuted as a concert pianist in Toronto (1952) and New York (1962), gave up his 25 year long piano concert-playing career (1965) although continuing to adjudicate until 1975; began lecturing throughout Canada, the USA and Europe promoting awareness of the individual's inherent freedom as a conscious being, a philosophy professing his strong musical interpretations; founded *Star-Scape Singers* (group of 10) who sing some of his over 3,000 poems set to originally composed music in Toronto, New York, Texas, Arizona and throughout Europe; is a recognized artist specializing in floral paintings in the acrylic medium and has exhibited in Canada and the US. *See:* **Arguing, Art, Change, Commitment, Creativity, Day, Eternal, Fidelity, Giving, Ideals, Inspiration, Intuition (× 3), Life, Limitations, Love (× 2), Miracle, Moment(s) (× 2). Nothing, Now, Possibilities, Present, Simplicity, Source, Soul, Voice, Wisdom (× 2), Wonder (× 2)**

MILTON, John (1608–1674) English poet, writer, pamphleteer, politician; he was writing odes, masques and elegies by 1638, was in Italy (1638–39) and returned to England on the brink of the Civil War; engaged in pamphleteering (1640–47) which produced a passionate appeal for freedom of the press; under Oliver Cromwell held the post as Secretary for Foreign Tongues (1649–1660) when he went blind; in 1658, he had begun his epic poetic masterpiece *Paradise Lost* (probably completed 1865); followed by *Paradise Regained* (1871) and others; in England and throughout Europe, these and his magnificent shorter poems gained popularity throughout the 18th and 19th centuries. *See:* **Childhood, Mind(s)**

MOZART, Wolfgang Amadeus (1756–1791) Austrian composer; showed an extra-ordinary and unique musical precocity, began to compose at the age of 5; in his short life, he produced a vast output and mastered all the musical forms of his time, was never rewarded for his talent during his lifetime, although his genius was recognized; his work includes 41 numbered symphonies, of which the last 3 are especially outstanding; concertos for piano, violin, French horn, etc., string quartets, sonatas, serenades and many other orchestral and chamber pieces, masses, hymns, musical religious songs, many operas including *The Marriage of Figaro* (1786), *Don Giovanni* (1787) and *The Magic Flute* (1791); he composed to a high degree of excellence with great speed and seemingly easily, but suffered from severe mood swings throughout his life, was probably a manic depressive (in modern terms) and died as the result of an episode when he had not eaten or slept for 72 hours (age 35); buried in a pauper's unmarked grave. *See:* **Love**

MURRAY, W. H. (1913–1986) Scottish; mountaineer, author and mountain rescue pioneer; began climbing Scottish mountains in 1936, with very primitive gear, and went on to write about his climbing adventures so vividly he inspired many young people to begin mountain-climbing; joined the Scottish Mountaineering Club (SMC) (1945, after end of World War II), was president of the SMC from 1962 and in 1989, Honorary President; active in conservation as an unpaid volunteer and Chairman of the Countryside Commission for Scotland (1968–1982) wrote *Undiscovered Scotland. See:* **Ego**

NAIR, Keshavan (Contemporary 1950±–?) American (USA) of Indian (East Indian) descent; writer, lecturer, seminar leader, psychologist, widely recognized expert on leadership and decision making; believes that creating trust in an organization makes practical business sense; espouses that a commitment to personal responsibility, not insistence on rights, should govern conduct and social policy in business as well as private life; believes that society loses respect for and trust in leaders based on their unacceptable conduct, public and private; his books include *Beyond Winning, The Handbook for the Leadership Revolution* (1988); *A Higher Standard of Leadership-Lessons from the Life of Gandhi* (1997) *The Soul of Business* (1997) and *Leadership for Special Challenges: Change, Diversity and Knowledge Organizations* (1990). *See:* **Courage**

NACHMANOVITCH, Stephen, Ph.D. (1906–1967) author, musician (violinist), educator and computer programmer and visual and sound computer artist (visual music tone painter, which is an art form employing sound, light and touch via electronic synthesizers turning music into a visual display); author of *Improvisation in Life and Art* (1991); *See:* **Muse**

NAPOLEON (Napoleon Bonaparte; Napoleon I, Emperor of the French (1769–1821) French Roman Catholic (Christian); solider, military commander, civil administrator, Emperor of France, writer; his life story was so impressive, it is now indistinguishable from legend; Napoleon was born to modest means on the Mediterranean Island of Corsica, decided on a military career at a young age and won a scholarship to a French military academy (1779); his military career began (1885) near the end of the historic French Revolution, in which the peasants revolted against the aristocracy and for many years looted, pillaged and destroyed the lives of the privileged, and sent many thousands of them to summary execution by the guillotine; married his wife Josephine (1796) and, his actual life notwithstanding, would have been remembered for his stormy, romantic and star-crossed love affair with her; he first conquered France in a coup d'état by over-throwing the Directory and establishing a relatively benevolent dictatorship, compared to the anarchy of the Revolutionaries (1799); established himself as chief consul and went on to subdue most of Europe; surprisingly, he was much respected and beloved by his soldiers and fellow officers; by plebiscite he was established as consul for life (1802) and crowned himself Emperor of France in the presence of the Pope (1804); his mete-oric rise in the military world to become one of the greatest military commanders in history astonished not only all of France but all of Europe and threatened the stability of the world; sometimes perceived as a ruthless power hungry conqueror, he denied this, arguing that he was a building a federation of free peoples in a Europe united under a liberal government; in the states he created (including a new France), he introduced con-stitutions, stabilized the currency (money system), incorporated law codes which encouraged religious freedom, abolished feudalism (and slave selfdom), created efficient governments and fostered education, science, literature and the arts; the most famous code, The Napoleonic French Civil Code of Law, still forms the basis of French (and French-Canadian in Quebec province) civil law; he appointed many of his relatives as viceroys or kings of other parts of Europe (including Germany, Holland, Spain and Italy), in part, he said to maintain civilized control of those countries; his first marriage was annulled and he married Marie Antoinette (1808); he invaded Russia (1812) but the Russian winter decimated his armies and many thousands died in the Russian cold; a new coalition against France was formed (1813) by Prussia, Russian, Britain, Sweden and

Austria and they were victorious over Napoleon at the Battle of the Nations (1813), forc-
ing Napoleon into exile on the Isle of Elba; King Louis XVIII regained the French throne
but Napoleon returned to fight again in (1815); he was finally defeated at the end of the
Hundred Days War at the Battle of Waterloo (1815), whereupon Napoleon was again
exiled, this time for life, to the Isle of Saint Helena where he spent his last days dictat-
ing his memoirs; Napoleon's personality and achievements remain subject of extreme
controversy, but his exceptional genius and tremendous impact on modern history are
not debatable; he died of cancer, and his body was returned to be entombed with hon-
our in Paris. *See:* **Harm**

NIETZSCHE, Friedrich Wilhelm (1844–1900) German philosopher, existentialist, his
brilliance was evidence early; became professor of philology at age 23 in Basel, Switzer-
land (1869–1879) leaving in ill health and was hopelessly insane by 1889 (age 45); his
work is characterized by enthusiastic love of life, has poetic and passionate grandeur but
shows a morbid sensitivity; has attracted many readers and his works are capable of
widely varying interpretations; the most important are aphorisms, essays and prose
poems, including *Thus Spake Zarasthustra* (1883, 1891) which condemns traditional Christ-
ian values as the code of the slavish masses and preaches superiority of the morality of
the masters (natural aristocrats) which arises from the will to power; essentially poetic
and symbolic, the book is obscure; other well known works are *The Birth of Tragedy* (1871)
and *Beyond Good and Evil* (1886); he was one of the major influences on 20th century
thought. *See:* **Addiction, Living, Pressure**

NIN, Ms Anais (1903–1977) French, born in Paris of a Canadian father and a Danish
mother; spent most of her earlier years with relatives in Cuba; later became a natural-
ized American (USA) citizen; lives and worked in Paris, New York and Los Angeles;
author of avante garde novels in the French surrealistic style, best known for self pub-
lished dairies, the *Dairy of Anais Nin*, Volumes I to VII (1966–1980) and *The Early Dairies of
Anais Nin*, Volumes I to IV (1978); she is appreciated for her erotica, the first woman to
really explore this genre; a friend of the writer Henry Miller. *See:* **Courage**

NORWOOD, Ms Robin (Contemporary 1960±–?) American (USA), author, psychologist; behavioural motivator, seminar leader, wrote, among other books: *Women Who Love Too Much; When You Keep Wishing and Hoping He'll Change.* (1985); *Tell Me Why This, Why Now— A Guide to Answering Life's Toughest Questions* (1995); *See:* **Recovery**

O'BRIEN, William (1852–1928) Irish journalist, parliamentarian and political leader and activist; one of the greatest 19th century parliamentarians; first elected to Parliament in 1881; at various times in his political career was in and out of jail for periods of 6 months of more, traveled for 6 months in Canada to raise for funds for his causes and fled to the USA to escape persecution at one point, but returned to be MP for Cork in 1902; his paper *United Ireland* championed agrarian reform; helped shape the *Wyndham Land Act* (1903) and *Amended Land Purchase Act* (1909) to solve The Irish Land Question (i.e., beginning in the 12th century and for 700 years, through a succession of political land confiscations by aristocracy and political leaders, ordinary Irish farmers had been precluded from owing the land they farmed; these acts for the first time guaranteed the farmers the 3 "Fs"—fair rent, fixity of tenure and freedom from sale and by 1921, Irish tenants owned ⅔ of the land, the rest was confiscated by law and given to the tenants), in 1910 he founded his *All For Ireland* movement but retired from politics in 1918; his writing include *When we were Boys* and *A Queen of Men. See:* **Promises**

ORIENTAL; *See also* **CONFUCIUS** *and* **Lao TSE** *in this list. See:* **Costs, Father**

ORUCLA *See:* **Heart**

OSLER, Sir William (1849–1919) Canadian physician, professor, lecturer, international medical pioneer and leader, medical historian, founder of medical libraries; throughout his life, helped develop and set the standards of modern medical practice; studied medicine at McGill University and after graduating and pursuing further studies in Europe; returned to McGill as a lecturer; in 1884 to 1889 moved to the University of Pennsylvania as Chair of Clinical Medicine, during which time he treated and was a friend of Walt Whitman, much loved American poet and editor; while there delivered a famous essay in which he urged graduating medical students to maintain imperturbability, an outward expression of calm and coolness while extending controlled empathy to patients, and to observe virtues of courage, patience and honesty; moved on to John Hopkins University and Hospital as Chief of Staff in 1889; was active in supporting and founding libraries including the Medical Library Association of which he became second president in 1901; in 1905 was appointed as Regius Professor of Medicine at Oxford University, England; wrote *The Principles and Practices of Medicine* and *Acquainimitas;* remained in England until his death in 1919. *See:* **Faith, Life**

OVERSTREET, H.A., B.A., B.S. (Harry Allen Overstreet) (1875–1970) American (USA) philosopher, writer, educator, instructor, lecturer; born in San Francisco; received his degrees at University of California, Berkeley (1899,1901); taught at Berkeley in philosophy (1901–1910); became Chair of the Department of Philosophy and Psychology at City College of New York (1911–1939); also taught in continuing education courses for the International Ladies' Garment Workers Union (1924–1936); lectured at Town Hall (New York) (1938) and was instrumental in the development of the serialized radio educational program "America's Town Meting of the Air"; authored *About Ourselves, Psychology for Normal People* (1927); co-authored with his second wife, Bonaro Wilkerson Overstreet, B.A., M.A. (also a poet, writer, philosopher and psychologist) *What We Must Know About Communism* (1958) which was a national best-seller and a study on the FBI, *Federal Bureau of Investigation in 1969; the FBI in our Open Society* (1969) which received wide-spread publicity. *See:* **Hate**

OVID (Publus Ovidius Naso) (43 B.C.–17 or 18 A.D.) Italian (Roman) poet; considered the last of the Golden Age poets (Vergil and Horace); came of age in the Augustian Age, the beginning of the Roman Empire; son of a locally prominent family, the Ovidi in Sulmona, the Paelignian area of Italy; earlier members of his family having held public office; the early death of his older brother made him the focus of his family's expectations so he was sent to Rome to be educated; studies rhetoric and embarked on a career in government; became administrator of the treasury and the prisons, then a judge and was on track for higher offices but chose poetry instead; began by writing love poetry and at least one early play; his greatest work was the epic *Metamorphoses;* 8 8 A.D., he was exiled but continued to write and during his lifetime enjoyed great literary success, later poets often imitating him. *See:* **Envy**

PASCAL, Blaise (1623–1662) French mathematician, scientist and religious philosopher/ apologist; the only son of 4 children, his mother died when he was 3 and his father (a civil servant) schooled him at home; at age 16, he invented the first digital calculator to help his father collect taxes; as a scientist, he laid the foundation for the modern theory of probabilities, invented syringe and the mathematical triangle (Pascal's triangle), advanced differential calculus and geometry; formulated studies of fluids and clarification of concepts such as pressure, vacuum and hydraulics, in 1654 (age 31) he nearly lost his life when the horses in a carriage in which he was a passenger plunged over the parapet of a bridge into the River Seine, but the carriage was left hanging off the bridge; at that point, he abandoned science entirely for philosophy and theology; his family had embraced Jansenism (Roman Catholic Christian sect which stressed personal holiness and austerity) and he wrote the ironic *Provincial Letters* (1656) in defense of Jansenism; his most famous religious writings collected in *Pensées* are considered unsurpassed examples of French classical prose, subtle, powerful and lucid, and argue for faith and the truth of Christianity versus free thinking or logic (1670), are profoundly mystical and considered very pure in literary style; he used his theory of probabilities to argue for the existence of God; Pascal died at age 39 in Paris in intense pain after a malignant growth in his stomach spread to his brain. *See:* **Heart**

PASTEUR, Louis (1822–1895) French chemist; through his with bacteria, he exploded the myth of spontaneous generation of disease; his work on wine, vinegar and beer lead to the process of pasteurization (a method of treating foods, especially milk, to make them free from disease-causing bacteria); he solved the problems of control of silkworm disease and chicken cholera; he developed a technique of vaccination against anthrax and extended it to hydrophobia; the Pasteur Institute, opened in 1888, includes clinic for treatments and teaching and a research center for virulent and contagious diseases; Pasteur Institutes have been opened in other countries. *See:* **Chance**

PAUL, Saint (also called Saul) (25±B.C.–67? A.D.) Jewish, Apostle to the Gentiles (of Jesus Christ), and the Books (Epistles) of the New Testament (Christian) attributed to him; one of the greatest figures in the Christian Church; one of the 12 Apostles/disciples of Jesus Christ; was originally a tentmaker by trade and a Roman citizen; educated in Jerusalem, he was a zealous Jewish nationalist; source of his history is Acts of the Apostles (New Testament) and the Epistles he wrote himself in various books of the New Testament; these Epistles (letters) are recognized as masterpieces of world literature as well as the foundation of the Christian doctrine; Saul converted to Paul was considered the greatest of the Christian missionaries; with different companions he traveled about the Near East and Greece, making conversions and setting up churches; in Jerusalem, he was accused or provoking a riot, was sent to jail for 2 years, after which he was sent to Rome (60–62 A.D.) where he was again imprisoned before being cleared of all charges; he apparently died under the persecution of Nero (Roman Caesar), traditionally on the same day as Saint Peter met the same fate, commemorated together on June 29th by Roman Catholics. *See:* **Anger**

PAULING, Linus, Ph.D. (1901–1994) American (USA) scientist, physicist, biochemist, natural health advocate, writer, lecturer, educator, pacifist; philosopher, the only person ever to receive two unshared Nobel Peace Prizes (for Chemistry in 1954 and Peace (1962); received the Gandhi and Lenin peace prizes, the Albert Schweitzer Peace medal; has been awarded honorary degrees by some 50 colleges and universities throughout the world; considered to be one of the two greatest scientists of the 20th century; born in Portland, Oregon; received his Ph.D. from California Institute of Technology (Caltech) in chemistry and mathematical physics; went to Europe (1926–27) where he studied the implications of quantum mechanics (for atomic structure); a string of scientific studies followed; joined faculty of Caltech (1927–1964); his introductory textbook *General Chemistry* (1947) has been revised 3 times, translated into 13 languages and has been used by generations of university students; his landmark book *The Nature of the Chemical Bond* is frequently cited as the most influential scientific book of the 20th century; considered a founding father of molecular biology, which has transformed the biological sciences and medicine; originated the concept of molecular disease, which became immensely important in finding new medical diagnosis and treatments and has led to the main focus on human genome research; with an associates, devised a synthetic form of blood plasma for blood transfusions; determined the cause of sickle cell anemia (the molecular disease prevalent among African-Amerians); was elected to the American Philosophical Society (1936); as a communicator, was eagerly sought as a speaker for conferences, political rallies, commencements and media programs; despite his general popularity and many awards, including a presidential one (1956), his pacifist political views in protesting against atmospheric nuclear testing were unpopular with the government of the US, his passport was confiscated (1950-54) denying him international travel, but when he won the Nobel Prize for Chemistry in 1954, it was promptly reinstated; helped found Center for the Study of Democratic Institutions (1942); later held professorships in chemistry of the University of California, San Diego (1967–69) and Stanford University (1969–73); outspoken about the importance of vitamins as early as the late 1930s, he founded the concept of orthomolecular medicine; he had a particular genius for translating difficult technical material into language understandable by intelligent lay persons, including *Vitamin C and the Common Cold* (1970); *Cancer and Vitamin C* and *How to Life Longer and Feel Better*; published over 1000 articles and books, about two-thirds on scientific subjects; founded the Linus Pauling Institute of Science and Medicine to conduct research in orthomolecular medicine (1973) following his belief that nutrition and vitamin supplementation could prevent, ameliorate or cure many diseases, slow the aging process and alleviate suffering; died at age 93, he is survived by 4 children, 15 grandchildren and 19 great-grandchildren. *See:* **Curiosity**

PEARCE, Joseph Chilton (1960±–?) American (USA) contemporary lecturer, inspirational speaker and leader; books include *The Biology of Transcendence: A Blueprint of the Human Spirit; The Crack in the Cosmic Egg: New Constructs of Mind and Reality; Magical Child;* and *Evolution's End: Claiming the Potential of our Intelligence. See:* **Creativity, Fear**

PETTLE, Alvin (1945–) graduated from the University of Toronto Medical School in 1969 and received his fellowship in Obstetrics and Gynecology in 1974. For 20 years he practised at the Etobicoke General Hospital where he delivered close to 10,000 babies in

Toronto. In the fall of 1994, his wife Carol and he opened up a women's wellness centre called the Ruth Pettle Wellness Centre in memory of his mother who died from breast cancer. Over the last ten years he has co-authored the book *Natural Remedies and Supplements*. He has also produced three audio CD's *The Natural Approach to P.M.S. and Menopause, When Bad Things Happen to Good People*, and *The Scientific Basis of Bio-Identical Hormones*. His video lectures include *12 Steps to Preventing Breast Cancer*. He continues his life work with Carol in Toronto, surrounded by their five children and six grandchildren.

PLATO (428?–348? B.C.) Greek philosopher; one of the most influential thinkers of all time, his writings, mostly in dialogue form, deal with virtue, mathematics, politics, beauty, the laws of thought, education, love, friendship, honor, etc.; born of a noble Athenian family, at age 20 he began study under Socrates, who appears as chief speaker in all of his early writings; traveled, stayed for a time in Syracuse, then returned to Athens where he founded the Academy (388) and taught for the rest of his life; his philosophy is expressed in his dialogues because he believed that man cannot find truth alone but must approach it through discussions; his written dialogues, because of their beauty of style as well as their depth and range of thought, are considered outstanding masterpieces of world literature; among his many writings are the *Apology, Symposium* and *Republic* (perhaps the most known, a demonstration of justice by picturing the ideal state); his teachings stressed and argued: that the importance of the idea, the general form, is the basis of true reality, permanent and sure behind all appearances; knowledge when true is eternal and unchangeable; the supreme Idea is the Idea of the Good; the rational soul is immortal; virtue consists of the harmony of the soul with the universe; all disorder is evil, including and especially in government; literature and art, the love of beauty lead to Goodness and virtue; Plato's chief pupil was Aristotle. *See:* **Exercise**

PLAUTUS, Titus Maccius (Titus Maccius/or Maccus) (254–184 B.C.) Italian (Roman) comic poet and playwrite; he adapted Greek comedies for the Roman stage; his 21 known plays include *Miles Gloriosus, Menaechmi, Amphitruo* and contain boisterous, low-comedy portrayals of middle-class and lower-class life, governed by a genius for situation and coarse humor and have characteristic stock figures; his influence on later European literature was enormous. *See:* **Doing**

PLAYER, Gary (1935–?) South African golfer, one of the most successful golfers in all time; third golfer in history to win the modern Golf Grand Slam; renowned as much for his dedication to the principles of excellence as he is for his golfing accomplishments, he is known world-wide as an uncompromising perfectionist who settles for nothing but the best; his impeccable set of values, stringent regimen of health and fitness and insistence on quality have earned him admiration all over the world. *See:* **Chance, Work**

PRATHER, Hugh (Contemporary 1945±–?) American (USA) Methodist (Christian Protestant) clergyman, author, crisis-counselor, pop-psychologist, self-help motivator; as a Minister for 30 years in his Foothills United Methodist Church, he has counseled couples, families in crisis, battered women and grieving parents who have lost their children; his first book, published by a small company with little advertising or promotion became a phenomenon when released; *Notes to Myself* (1970) has sold more than 5 million copies and has been translated into 10 languages; often in collaboration with his wife, Gayle, he has written a string of more than 40 self-help books since which have given inspiration and insight to millions of people around the world; including: *The Little Book of Letting Go; I Will Never Leave You; Notes on How to Live in the World . . . . and Still Be Happy; Notes on Love and Courage; Parables from Other Planets* and *There is a Place Where You Are Not Alone;* he is the father of 3 sons. *See:* **Ambition, Anger, Communication, Expectations, Father, Fear, Friendship, Guilt, Honesty, Humor, Hurting, Love (× 4), Now (× 3), Opinion, People, Silence, Soul, Spiritual, Work, Worry**

PROUST, Marcel (1871–1922) French novelist, when young he sought the company of fashionable and intellectual society, in his seven semi-autobiographical novels entitled *A la recherche du temps perdu"* (1913–27) and *Remembrance of Things Past* (1922–32), he recreates in fictional form his youth in Paris and the Normandy countryside; in effect recreating the upper-class French society at the turn of the century; certain themes emerge, above all that of the transforming power of dominant love, the effects it has on the lover's vision of the beloved and the world, but in another sense the transformation of the universe by the individual perceiving and suffering it; his complicated style seeks by total recall to recapture the smallest psychological and sensory details and reflects the characteristics of personal vision, is highly poetic and full of elaborate imagery; his works had a profound influence on the art of novel writing. *See:* **Addiction**

PROVERBS (986–932 B.C.?) book of the Torah (Jewish) or Old Testament Bible (Christian), a collection of didactic sayings, many of them moral maxims, mostly ascribed by tradition to Solomon; the book is an early example of wisdom literature popular among Jews of post-exilic time; a proverb in modern common use is a brief, familiar maxim of folk wisdom, often involving a bold image and frequently a jingle that catches the memory to illustrate and enhance a moral opinion; modern scholars dispute the sole origin of the Proverbs to Solomon. *See also* **SOLOMON** *in this list. See:* **Work**

PSALMS (972 B.C.) book of the Torah (Jewish) or Old Testament Bible (Christian), a collection of 150 poetic pieces, the historical first hymnal of Jews and Christians; many of the psalms traditionally ascribed to King David, a shepherd boy who became King of the Jews by overcoming Goliath with a sling-shot, a Hebrew national hero celebrated not only for his valour as a warrior but his ability as a ruler and his gifts as a poet and musician; some are penitential poems, some express the poet's reverence for God; Psalms have been translated into more languages and in greater varieties of form than any other Book of the Old Testament Bible. *See:* **Dad, God, Gossip**

PTALLOTOPE (2350 B.C.) *See:* **Time**

RABELAIS, François, M.D. (1490–1553) French, Benedictine Roman Catholic Christian, physician, monk, author, satirist; took a medical degree at Montpellier where he later also taught; while at Lyons (1532–34) he wrote his satirical romances *Gargantua* and *Pantagruel,* the first a history of a giant and the second the history of the giant's son; third and fourth books followed (1546–52); under its burlesque, sometimes ribald, humour, these stories conceal serious considerations of education, politics and philosophy; although his name became synonymous with "coarse, vulgar, earthy humour," he is also noted for his breadth of learning, his zest for living and his humanistic outlook; his work is primarily a satire against the abuses of society; after the death of his patron, King Francis I, he spent his last days as a priest at Meudon. *See:* **Wisdom**

REDDY, Helen (Contemporary 1950±–?) Australian, singer, entertainer; born into a well-known Australian show-business family, after coming to the USA in her early 20s, she signed with Capitol Records; the first track she cut was not only her first hit single but also the first hit single for Andrew Lloyd Webber, *I Don't Know How to Love Him;* however, it was the song she wrote herself, *I Am Woman,* that became her first number one record; she won a Grammy award for her performance and the song is now recognized as the anthem for the feminist movement; more than ten notable singles follows, including: *Leave Me Alone, Angie Baby, Delta Dawn, You and Me Against the World,* all gold or platinum selling albums leading to her international multi-media career; her starring role in the Disney film, *Pete's Dragon,* continues to attract a new generation of fans; performs in stage plays of *Anything Goes, Call Me Madam, The Mystery of Edwin Drood* and others; active in community affairs, she served for 3 years as Commissioner of Parks and Recreation for the State of California; has received many honours, including a tulip named in her honour in Holland. *See:* **Woman**

RICE, Grantland (1880–1954) American (USA) sportswriter, reporter, poet, magazine and book writer, film producer, war veteran, philanthropic fund-raiser; book about him: *How You Played the Game—The Life of Grantland Rice* by William Harper (1999); *See:* **Winning**

ROCHEFOUCAULD, due la François (1613–1680) French writer, known for his moral maxims and reflective epigrams; born heir to an ancient family; known in his youth as prince de Marcillac, although he owned extensive estates in Angomois, he settled in Paris (1652) and was part of their leading literary circles; his pessimistic philosophy was that selfishness is the source of all human behaviour; his *Reflexions ou sentences et maximes morales,* a collection of witty, polished and clever maxims (concise statements of doctrine or opinion) were published 5 times during his lifetime (the fifth edition containing 504 maxims); several translations of this work into English, one by Louis Kronenberger (1959); also wrote his own *Memoirs; See:* **Self**

REBBE (The) (Menachem Mendel Schneerson) (1902–1994) Ukrainian birth, naturalized American (USA) citizen; sage, visionary, spiritual leader, awarded the Congressional

Gold Medal (USA) for his outstanding contributions towards education, morality and acts of charity; Rabbi for 44 years of the Lubavitch movement of Chassidus Jewish group centered in Brooklyn, New York, believed by many of his followers to be the Messiah or long expected messenger directly from God and hence called by them, *The Rebbe*; born in the Ukraine, the son of a scholarly Rabbi; in early childhood was noted for his extra-ordinary mental abilities; left school for private tutoring; by the age of bar mitzvah (13), he was considered a prodigy of Torah (instruction books of the Jewish faith); studied religion throughout his life; married a daughter of the former leader of the Lubavitch movement in 1928; lived and studied in Berlin (1928–1933) studying mathematics and science, continuing at the Sorbonne in Paris (1933–1941) before fleeing German-occupied France for the USA (1941); in 1950 (age 48) on the death of his father-in-law, assumed leadership of the Lubavitch movement, which had been reduced by Jewish deaths in World War II to a small number of faithful; grew with the Rabbi's leadership to 200,000 persons worldwide by 1994; there are now 1,400 institutions in 35 countries on 6 continents, world-wide; he taught in Yiddish, which was translated by his followers into Hebrew, English and other languages; although Jewish, his teaching was of a universal nature, calling on all mankind to lead productive and virtuous lives, which will lead to personal redemption; for unity between all people, that God created the universe with the intention that mankind would civilize and perfect it; he established education and outreach centres, offering social service programs and humanitarian aid to all people, regardless of religious affiliation; by blending traditional religious training with deep compassion and insight and modern positive psychological thinking, he became a leader deeply respected by those in politics and business as well as religion; his literary output was prodigious, including hundreds of essays and over 200,000 letters to people around the world; many books have been written about him and his teachings and translated into English and other languages, including *Toward a Meaningful Life*, adapted by Simon Jacobson, who for 14 years (1977–1994) prepared the Rebbe's talks for publication and has gathered together a representative collection of his teachings; died of a stroke and heart attack in his 92nd year. *See:* **Addiction, Advice (× 2), Aura, Awakened, Bad Times, Birth (× 2), Consciousness, Death (× 2), Destiny, Differences, Dignity, Doing, Education, Emotions (× 3), Failure, Faith, Gambling, God, Good-**

ness (× 2), Growth, Healing, Heart, Home, Knowledge, Life (× 3), Light, Love (× 2), Meaning (× 2), Mind(s), Sharing, Silencer, Soul, Struggle, Success, Suffering, Synchronicity, Time (× 3), World, Words (× 5)

ROETHKE, Theodore (1908–1963) American (USA) poet, writer, philosopher, awarded Pulitzer Price for poetry in 1954 for his book, *The Waking;* son of a German immigrant who with his brother owned and operated a greenhouse operation, he spent much of his childhood in and around greenhouses and plants, and much of his work illustrates his extensive knowledge of this world; attended the University of Michigan and Harvard but did not graduate; he suffered bipolar disorder throughout his adult life, for which he was hospitalized, and had bouts with alcohol addiction, the psychology of which he discusses in some of his work; his first book took 10 years to write, *Open House* (1941); stylistically, his work ranged from witty poems in strict meter and regular stanzas to lyrical free verse poems full of mystical and surrealistic imagery, at all times reflecting the natural world with its beauty, mystery, fierceness and sensuality. *See:* **Depression, Learning, Mind(s)**

ROLLIN, Charles (1661–1741) French theologian, professor, administrator, historian, writer; follower of Jansenism (a Roman Catholic Christian doctrine founded by the Dutch monk, Jensen, which was very popular in France); son of a cutler (one who makes and sells knives and scissors), intended to follow his father's trade, but because of his piety secured a collegiate scholarship; studied theology but was never ordained; professor of rhetoric (effective persuasive language), of Latin eloquence (1688) at several colleges; at age 33 appointed rector of the university and later principal of a college (1696–1722); began writing after his retirement (age 61); his many books (in French) reflect talented language facility and enthusiasm, a pure and upright conscience, sweet humor and his own personal robust good health. *See:* **Heights**

ROOSEVELT, Eleanor (Anna Eleanor Roosevelt) (1884–1962) American (USA), First Lady, orator, author and social activist; she married her cousin, Franklin D. Roosevelt (32nd President of the United States of America, 1933–1945) and when he became crippled by polio (1921) she represented him on the campaign trail; as First Lady she undertook special causes, especially youth employment and civil rights for minorities, and continued working for these causes after her husband's death; was USA delegate to the United Nations (1945–1952, 1961–1962) and was considered instrumental in drafting the International Declaration of Human Rights; wrote *This I Remember* (1949) and *The Autobiography of Eleanor Roosevelt* (1961). *See:* **Personality**

ROOSEVELT, Theodore (1858–1919) American (USA); soldier, writer, politician, naturalist, historian, 26th President of the United States of America (Republican) (1901–1909); considered one of the greatest and most outspoken Presidents in American history; awarded Nobel Peace Prize (1906) for his mediation in the Russo-Japanese was (1904–05); born New York City and considered frail as a child, he set out to build his strength as a young man; Assistant Secretary of the Navy (1897–98), he left to organize and lead a famous Regiment of volunteers known as the Rough Riders; as a colonel cavalry officer in Cuba (1898); Governor of New York State (1899–1900); U.S. Vice-President (1901); became President on the assassination of President McKinley (1901); as president organized trust-busting campaign, vigorously championing the rights of ordinary men versus corporate power; promoted conservation of natural resources; pushed the Monroe Doctrine allowing the USA to interfere in the affairs of Latin American countries as a super police power, called the "big-stick" policy; pursued dollar diplomacy of other countries, notably in the Caribbean; used the U.S. Navy to ensure that Panama gained independence from Columbia and secured the right to construct the Panama Canal; engaged in hunting and exploring expeditions throughout his career; had a ranch in the Dakotas; wrote many books dealing with history, travel, politics, hunting, wildlife, his essays and addresses during political office, a collection of more than 20 years of letters with his children. *See:* **Success, Work**

ROUSSEAU, Jean Jacques (1712–1778) French philosopher, romanticist, essayist, novelist, writer, musical theorist and composer; born Geneva, Switzerland; his wandering and troubled life was made tolerable only by his many patrons and protectors, of both sexes, one of whom was his mistress in France; his volatile emotions, tendency to argue with everyone about virtually everything and daring statements got him into trouble with authorities in both France and Switzerland, and he had to flee to Germany and then (1765) to England; became increasingly paranoid as he grew older; may or may not have fathered 5 children (whom he said were all put into foster homes) by his common-law English wife/protector; among his essays he glorifies nature (including human nature) and contends that man is naturally good but corrupted by civilization; drafted constitutions for Corsica and Poland (neither of which was implemented); had very complex ideas and was considered one of the major 18th century influences on shaping romanticism and later philosophical thought; believed man was a pure animal, neither good nor bad; the child should be able to develop without interference; favored feeling and emotion against reason; equality between people disappeared with the introduction of property, agriculture and industries; laws were made to preserve inequalities; his book, *Confessions*, published posthumously, was one of the most celebrated auto-biographies ever written; his competence in music was self-taught. *See:* **Doing, Imagination**

ROSSETTI, Christina (Christina Georgina Rossetti) (1830–1894) English poet, writer (sister to Dante Rossetti (1828–1882) British writer known for his sonnets); lived as a recluse for 15 years; Pre-Raphaelite; her work, mainly lyrical is combined with a strong element of mystical or religious feeling; had a sense for colour and atmosphere; published several books, including *Goblin Market and Other Poems* (1862). **See: Memory**

ROSTAND, Edmond (1868–1918) French playwright, dramatist; wrote *Cyrano de Bergerac* (1897) and *l'Aiglon* (1900); his best known works are distinguished by wit and brilliance. **See: Now Moments**

RUNYON, Damon (Alfred Damon Runyon) (1884–1946) American (USA) writer of short stories, notably *Guys and Dolls* (1931), *Blue Plate Special* (1934) and *Money From Home* (1935) which portray underworld characters in New York City. *See:* **Winnings**

RUSKIN, John (1819–1900) English art critic, essayist, lecturer; made his name as an art critic with the first part of *Modern Painters* (1843), began as a defence of Turner; visits to

Switzerland and Italy (especially Venice) led to *The Seven Lamps of Architecture* (1849) and *The Stones of Venice* (1851–53); *Modern Painters* continued to appear until 1860; in 1853, Ruskin began his career as a lecturer, mainly in art, but later on economic, social and general social issues; further works follows, including an autobiography; as an art critic, he had little use for contemporary art; as a social critic, he emphasized the distinction between mere wealth and true social welfare, and between mechanical labour and craftsmanship; was a critic of the new industrial society; *See:* **Rewards, Work**

RUSSELL, Bertrand, 3rd Earl Russell of Bedford (Bertrand Arthur William Russell) (1872–1970) English philosopher and mathematician; descendant of a long historical English noble family tracing its nobility to 1486 at the time of Henry VIII; with N.A. Whitehead, co-authored *Principia Mathematica* (1910–13); a pioneer work in symbolic logic; other writings include *An Outline of Philosophy* (1927) and *Philosophy and Politics* (1947); a realist, his object was to give philosophy a scientific basis; as a social thinker, he stresses creative activity of man, which he calls the principle of growth; won the Nobel Prize for Literature (1950) *See:* **Wisdom**

SAHARA *See:* **Body**

SANSKRIT (2nd millennium B.C.) one of the official languages of India; it occupied (and still does) a role similar to Latin; it was and still is the language of religious ritual and scholarship; has locally varied spoken forms; there are several times more documents preserved in Sanskrit than in Latin; in its oldest Vedic form, it is a close descendant of Indo-European root language and is practically identical to Zorastrianism (also the oldest recorded religion in the world); intense study of Sanskrit around 100 B.C. marked the beginnings of linguistics (study of language); oldest known grammar book in Sanskrit dates to approximately 500 B.C. *See also* **BUDDHA** *in this list. See:* **New Moments**

SARTON, Mary *See:* **Truth**

SCHAFF, Anne Wilson *See:* **Yourself**

SCHNEERSON, Menachem Mendel; *See (The) REBBE, in this list.*

SCHOPENHAUER, Arthur (1788–1860) German philosopher; in *The World as Will and Idea* (1818), he stated that the will is the key to reason; his statement that without the will "before us there is nothing" is regarded as a classic expression of pessimism; he espoused Buddhism and a world-denying mysticism as superior to then current Christian theology. *See:* **Time**

SCHWECK, C. *See:* **Personality**

SENECA, Lucius Anneus (4 B.C.–65 A.D.) Italian (Roman) philosopher, tutor, dramatist, essayist, satirist, statesman; exiled by Roman Emperor Claudius (41 A.D.), he was recalled to tutor Nero and was an advisor during the early of Emperor Nero's reign; later, implicated in a conspiracy to murder Nero and in disgrace, he was forced to commit suicide by slitting his wrists; his death was considered noble by Romans; he wrote satire and stoic essays on ethics and philosophy but his 9 tragedies, including *Medea, Agamemnon* and *Oedipus,* contrived but high-toned, are considered classics of literature and were very influential in the Renaissance era and later European development. *See:* **Desire, Difficulty**

SHAKESPEARE, William (1564–1616) English, considered a towering genius and greatest of English speaking poets, authors and dramatists, tragedian, writer of comedies and plays, social satirist, producer, theatre owner, historian, possibly schoolmaster; born Stratford-Upon-Avon; little is known of his early or personal life but many theories exist; he was well educated, may have been a schoolmaster; In 1582 married and had three children; by 1588 had moved to London and became involved in theatre, probably as an apprentice; by 1589 his first drama was produced, either *A Comedy of Errors* or the first part of *Henry VI;* continued to produce popular plays in a steady stream until his retirement (1610) with a modest fortune; part owner of theatres, the Globe and Blackfriars; most scholars accept 38 plays as being by him (partially or wholly); much speculation but no proof exists that he was really Francis Bacon or the Earl of Oxford; some of his well-known popular plays still being performed today include: *The Two Gentlemen of Verona;*

Love;'s Labour's Lost; The Taming of the Shrew; King John; Richard II, A Midsummer Night's Dream; The Merchant of Venice; Romeo and Juliet; The Merry Wives of Windsor; Much Ado About Nothing; Julius Caesar; Twelfth Night; All's Well That Ends Well; Hamlet; Othello; King Lear; MacBeth; Antony and Cleopatra; The Tempest and *Henry VIII;* his poetry, at times majestic, at times lyric, at times incredibly witty, has an incomparable excellence, yet without his plays he would have been remembered separately for his sonnets (1593–96); all ages since his have admired his command of language; he is presented by modern critics as deeply concerned with the moral basis of life; nature, right, order, truth appear to have been his key concepts. *See:* **Doing**

SHAW, George Bernard (1856–1950) Irish socialist, dramatist, playwright, dramatic and music critic; won 1925 Novel Prize for Literature; born Dublin; went to London where he wrote 5 little-known novels; became music critic (1888–1890), a dramatic critic (1895); long interested in economics and socialism, he was an early member of the Fabian Society (who repudiated Marxist class struggle, believing in natural development of socialism); his major plays include *The Devil's Disciple* (1896), *Caesar and Cleopatra* (1899), *Captain Brassbound's Conversation* (1899), *Man and Superman* (1903), *Major Barbara* (1905), *The Doctor's Dilemma* (1906), *Androcles and the Lion* (1911), *Pygmylion* (1912), his masterpiece *Saint Joan* (1924); he also wrote essays on widely divergent subjects including *The Intelligent Woman's Guide to Socialism and Capitalism* (1928); his complete works were published in 1930–32 in 30 volumes; considered a great theatrical craftsman, he was known to express himself on all subjects with great frankness, sometimes with wisdom, always with wit. *See:* **Dreams, Light**

SHELLEY, Mary (1797–1851) English romantic novelist, best known as the writer of *Frankenstein* or *The Modern Prometheus* (1818); born in London, her mother died when she was 10 days old; daughter of the writer and political journalist William Godwin; her father had revolutionary attitudes to most social institutions including marriage and education; as a child, she was left to educate herself amongst her father's intellectual circle (who included Hazlett, Lamb, Coleridge and Percy Shelley); her father took a second wife (1801) but Mary never grew to like her; she published her first poem at age 10, ran away to France and Switzerland with Percy Shelley at age 16; they eloped and married (1816) after Shelley's first wife (with whom he had eloped 3 years prior) committed suicide by drowning; their first child, a daughter, died in Venice few years later and their son, William, died of malaria at the age of 3, after which Mary had a nervous breakdown (1819); in 1822, she suffered a dangerous miscarriage and the same year, Percy Shelley drowned during a storm; of their children, only one survived infancy; the story of Frankenstein was written on a challenge to write a ghost story by Lord George Byron, whom she met while on a trip to Switzerland, and with the encouragement of her husband, the book was written within a year; the story of Frankenstein's monster has inspired over 50 films. *See:* **Writing**

SMILES, Samuel (1812–1904) Scottish surgeon, reformer, author (historical, political, biographical, and self-help), newspaper editor, secretary for a railway company; born one of 11 children left fatherless in 1832 (he was 20) he learned the meaning of self-reliance, his father was a shopkeeper but he qualified in medicine (and surgery) at Edinburgh University; devoted his leisure time to the advocacy of political and social reform; wrote biographies of industrial leaders and humble self-taught students; best known for his book, *Self-Help* (1859) which enshrined the Victorian values of success through hard work and was translated into many languages; the book preached industry, thrift and self-improvement and attacked "over-government"—has been criticized by some as a work that symbolized the ethics and aspirations of mid-19th century bourgeois individualism; titles of his other works on similar themes such as *Character, Thrift, Duty* (1880) are self-explanatory. *See:* **Helping**

SMITH, Sydney (1771–1845) English clergyman (Church of England Protestant Christian), noted as the wittiest man of his time; educated at Winchester and Oxford; went to Edinburgh (Scotland) to be the tutor to the son of an English gentleman; where there he proposed the founding of and helped establish the *Edinburgh Review*, for which he continued to write for the next 25 years; his *Peter Plymley Letters* in defense of Catholic emancipation, promoted religious toleration, an example of his defense of the oppressed; as a preacher, he was kindly and philanthropic, a hater of mysticism; his political writing was the most tolerant of reform of his time; his wit, while spontaneous and exuberant, was always used with careful consideration for the feelings of others; his honesty and sincerity were obvious and his personality was as winning as it was amusing; *See:* **Self**

SOLOMON (986–932 B.C.) *See also* **PSALMS** *and* **ECCLESIASTES** *in this list, (of which he is reputed author)* Israeli, Jewish, King of the Hebrews (972–932 B.C.), son of King David; (this name in Hebrew means "peaceful"); famous for his wisdom and his wealth; the bright side of his reign was characterized by peace, commercial expansion (he established foreign alliances and made trade agreements) and intensive building (i.e., the Temple at Jerusalem), the dark side by extravagance, heavy taxes and rising discontent among the northern tribes; several books of the Torah (Jewish) or Bible (Christian Old Testament of the Bible) are traditionally ascribed to him: Proverbs, Ecclesiastes, Wisdom and Song of Solomon (although modern scholars dispute these authorships); in popular legend, Solomon is the figure of the wise man and also the husband of many wives. *See also* **ECCLESIASTES** *in this list. See:* **Love**

SOPHOCLES (496–406 B.C.) Green tragic poet, gained first dramatic triumph in 468 B.C. and thereafter did so about 20 times; in developing new style drama, he added a third actor, developed scene painting and modified dramatic form and extended the range of human emotion that was expressed in plays, his characters existed on a more human level than previously and govern their own fate by their own faults, rather than by the actions of the gods; author of 123 plays, of which 7 complete plays survive, among them *Ajax, Antigone, Electra, Oedipus Rex,* or *Odiepus Tyrannus* (in which dramatic irony reaches an apex, cited by Aristotle as a perfect example of tragedy). *See:* **Looking**

SPINOZA, Baruch (1632–1677) Dutch philosopher, author; in *Tractatus* (1670) and *Ethics* (1677), he develops religious rationalism, written in a strictly mathematical form, expounding a theory of human salvation as knowledge of God, and also analyses the human soul; his system is a pantheistic doctrine according to which God is a substance constituted by an infinity of attributes of which we know only two: thought and extension; he was a firm believer of political democracy as a reflection of reason. *See:* **Understanding**

STANHOPE, Philip Dormer, Earl of Chesterfield (1694–1773) English statesman, parliamentarian, was in charge of foreign affairs (1714–17, 1718–21) and was first lord of the treasury (1717–18); author of worldly-wise *Letters to His Son* (1774) advice addressed to his natural son. *See:* **Doing, Knowledge**

STANLEY, Bessie Anderson (Bessie Anderson Stanley, Mrs. Arthur J. Stanley) (1879–19--) author of a quotation reprinted by the syndicated advice columnist Ann Landers in her column March 11, 1995; which begins: "He has achieved success who has lived well, laughed often and loved much ..."; the quotation was entered and originally won a $250 cash prize for Mrs. Stanley in 1904 in a contest held by the *Brown Book Magazine*; she used the funds to pay off the mortgage on her home, among other things, as reported by her great-granddaughter (Beth-Anne Larson) in August of 2001; her husband was Federal Judge Arthur J. Stanley (1902–2001) who during his lifetime authenticated Mrs. Stanley as the author of the passage; this quotation often miscredited to Ralph Waldo Emerson. *See:* **Success**

STEVENSON, Robert Louis (1850–94) English novelist, poet and essayist; a life-long victim of tuberculosis, he travelled much in search of health; began writing essays (1876); wrote many short stories and travel books such as *Travelling with a Donkey In Cévennes;* on a trip to California (1879) he married, returning to England (1880); his famous books, still avidly read, include *Treasure Island* (1883), *A Child's Garden of Verses* (1885), *Kidnapped* and *The Strange Case of Dr. Jekyl and Mr. Hyde* (both 1886); he went to Saranac Lake in New York state, where he began *The Master of Ballantrae* (1887); he made an extensive tour of the South Seas (1889), then settled down on his estate, in Samoa, to write *Weir of Hermison* (1896) and *St. Ives* (1897) were unfinished at his death (age 44); *See:* **Soul**

SWANN, T. (Thomas Burnett Swann) (1928–1976) American (usa) poet, academic and science fiction writer whose first published science fiction was *Winged Victory* for *Fantastic Universe Magazine* in 1958; a large body of science fiction short stories and novels followed, including: *The Day of the Minotaur* (1966), *Moondust* (1968), *The Dolphin and the Deep* (1968), *How are the Mighty Fallen* (1974), *Cry Silver Bells* (1977); *See:* **Aging**

SWIFT, Jonathon (1667–1745) Irish theologian, satirist; political activist; Roman Catholic (Christian), Dean of St. Patrick's Cathedral, Dublin; wrote *Gulliver's Travels* (1726) a children's classic, originally intended as a non-fiction satire on courtly life, politics, academism and mankind in general; *Tale of a Tub* (1704) a satire on the history of the Christian religion; *The Battle of the Books* (1704) and *Drapier's Letters* (1724) which had an enormous political effect; *The Modest Proposal* (1729) which emphasized his personal horror of human life and sense of terror and imbalance. *See:* **Now Moments**

SYRUS, PUBLILIUS (also known as Publus Syrus) (1st century B.C.); Roman (Italian); slave, mime, entertainer, a slave brought to Rome some years before the downfall of the Roman Empire, who became highly celebrated as a mimographer; said to have flourished around 45 B.C.; a compilation containing many lines of his original mimes is still available under the title *Publii Syri Sententaie; See:* **Speech**

SZENT-GYORGYI, Albert von (Albert von Nagyrapolt Szent-Gyorgyi) (1893–1986) Hungarian biochemist, won Novel Prize in Physiology and Medicine (1937) for pioneer work on biological oxidation and ascorbic acid (Vitamin C); he isolated Vitamin C and prepared it in bulk from paprika. *See:* **Discovery**

TALMUD (The) (Palestinian Talmud, compiled 400; Babylonian Talmud compiled 600) the vast collection of ancient rabbinic writings (taken from oral sources and tradition) on Jewish law and tradition; contains two sections: (1) the Mishna, or text of the Oral Law (in Hebrew) and (2) the Gemara, a commentary on the Mishna (in Aramaic), which it supplements; together they constitute the basis of religious authority in Orthodox Judaism; considered an authoritative record of discussions on Jewish laws, ethics, customs, legends and stories; written records first produced under the direction of Juda ha-Nasi (sometimes referred to as The Rebbe); based upon the expositions of the law by Hillel and Shammai, etc. In the Middle Ages, thousands of Talmudic manuscripts were destroyed by the Christians; the term Talmud is sometimes used to refer to the Germara alone. *See also* **HILLEL** *in this list. See:* **Growth**

THOMAS A. KEMPIS; X-Reference — *See KEMPIS, Thomas A. in this list.*

THOMAS, LEWIS, M.D. (1913–1993) American (USA), medical doctor, administrator, scientific author, essayist, journalist, educator; born New York state, son or a surgeon, graduate from Princeton and Harvard Universities (M.D.); member National Academy of Sciences; was Dean of medical school at Yale and New York Universities; winner National Book Award for *The Lives of a Cell—Notes of a Biology Watcher* (1974); also wrote, among others: *Medusa and the Snail* (1979), *The Fragile Species (Man)* (1992), comments from the career of a 50-year medical doctor; *See:* **Worry**

THOREAU, Henry David (1817–1862) American (USA) naturalist, author, social critic, essayist; American Transcendentalist (individual thinker); was a friend of Ralph Waldo Emerson, Margaret Fuller, Louisa May Alcott), best known for *Walden* (1854), an account of his living alone at Walden Pond, near Concord Massachusetts, to observe the life of the woods; also wrote *A Week on the Concord and Mirrimack Rivers* (1849), *The Maine Woods* (1863) and *Cape Cod 1865);* a powerful social critic, he was disturbed by the trend of Western civilization towards industrial urban society dominated by the profit motive; his essay *On The Duty of Civil Disobedience* (1849) inspired such later social activists as Mahatma Gandhi; more famous now than in his own time, his ideas have been widely influential. *See:* **Aspirations, Confidence, Cost, Life, Self, Work**

TILLICH, Paul Johannes (1886–1965) American (USA) theologian (Christian Protestant), author; incorporated depth psychology into Christian doctrine postulating that faith is "ultimate concern," that God is the "ground of being," and that man should strive for a "new being" rather than "salvation." *See:* **Destiny**

TOLSTOY, Leo N., Count (Count Lev Nikolayevitch Tolstoy) (1828–1910) Russian novelist, soldier and religious philosopher; born to a rich and noble family; served as an officer in the Caucasus Campaign and the Crimean War; in 1849 and 1859 attempted to open schools for illiterate serfs; early biographical works, *Childhood* (1852), *Boyhood* (1854) and *Youth* (1857) began his literary career; trips to the West (1857 and 1860) led him to question the basis for western civilization; after marriage (1862) he retired to his estate, Yasnaya Polyana where he wrote *The Cossacks* (1863) and *War and Peace* (1864–1869), a prose epic of the Napoleonic War, considered by many as the finest novel ever written, *Anna Karenina* (1875–1877), a moral tragedy against the backdrop of St. Petersburg society, *The Death of Ivan Ilyich* (1884) and lesser works; by 1876, he underwent a religious conversation to belief in Christian love, nonresistance to evil and the simple faith of the peasants, rejected the institutions, broke up with his wife, gave away his personal property and died in poverty at a railroad station, accompanied only by his daughter, Alexandria. *See:* **Change, Faith**

TWAIN, Mark (pseudonym for Samuel Longhorne Clemens) (1835–1910) American (USA) humorist, author, journalist, social activist; known as America's greatest story-teller and most widely read of American writers; after youth in Hannibal, Missouri, he was a pilot/navigator on the Mississippi River until the Civil War (1861–1865) and took his pen name from the leadsman's call ("mark twain" means two fathoms sounded); in 1862, wrote for the Virginia City *Enterprise;* first won fame (1865) for his story *The Celebrated Jumping Frog of Calaveras County;* a trip to the Holy Land led to his very popular *Innocents Abroad* (1869); after marriage (1870) he settled in New York and then Connecticut; he wrote his masterly recreations of his boyhood, *The Adventures of Tom Sawyer* (1876) and *The Adventures of Huckleberry Finn* (1884); also wrote many popular works including *A Tramp Abroad* (1879), *Life on the Mississippi* (1883) and two novels, *The Prince and the Pauper* (1880) and *A Connecticut Yankee in King Arthur's Court* (1889); plunged into debt by unfortunate investments (1893), he then lectured his way around the world; saddened by the death of both of his daughters and his wife, his later works were more pessimistic. *See:* **Death**

TSU, Lao (Old Master) (604 B.C.) Chinese, sage, philosopher, writer; legendary founder of the philosophy known as Taoism; Lao Tsu was not his actual name, but an honorary title, meaning *Old Master;* worked as a librarian in the Imperial library of the state court; was said to have traveled widely in China (and maybe outside); during his lifetime, refused to write his teachings during as he did not want them to turn into formal dogma; Lao Tsu's philosophy was to live life in an instinctive way with goodness, serenity and respect for all; he laid down no rigid code of behavior; he believed a person's conduct should be governed by instinct and conscience; that simplicity is the key to truth and freedom, man to achieve Tao must give up all strivings, his highest goal to escape from the illusion of desire through mystical contemplation. Legend says that near the end of his life he set off into the desert to leave civilization behind; when he got to the final gate at the great wall that protected the kingdom, the gatekeeper (a disciple) persuaded him to record the principles of his philosophy for posterity, the result being the 81 rhymed (in Chinese) sayings of the *Tao-Te-Ching* (*Tao* meaning the natural way of life, *Te* meaning the fit use of life by men and *Ching* meaning text or classic); (Tao is also spelled Dao); this ancient Chinese text is the world's most translated classic next to the Bible. *See:* **Self**

VAN DYKE, Henry (1852–1933) American (USA) clergyman, educator, U.S. Ambassador and inspirational poet, author and essayist; Christian (Presbyterian); born in Pennsylvania, educated at Princeton; pastor in New York City (1830–1899), professor or English literature, Princeton (1899–1923), U.S. Minister to the Netherlands (1913–1916); among his writings is the Christmas story *The Other Wise Man* (1896); his poetry and essays in *Little Rivers* (1895) and *Fisherman's Luck* (1899); *See:* **Talent**

VIRGIL (Publius Virgilius Maro) (70–19 B.C.) Italian (Latin) poet, patronized by the Emperors Maecenas and Augustus, he was able to spend his entire life creating poetry and was the foremost poet of his age; a collection of pastoral poems, wrote: *Eclogues* (43–37 B.C.) and *Georgics* (37–30 B.C.), a series of poems on the art of farming; the remaining 11 years of his life were spent composing *Aeneids*, glorifying the history of the Roman Empire; considered a model poet and was widely imitated throughout the Latin speaking period (to 1600 A.D.), including by Dante (1265–1321) who wrote *The Divine Comedy. See:* **Will**

VOLTAIRE, François M.A. (François Marie Arouet de Voltaire) (1694–1778) French philosopher, man of letters, playwright, author and historian; whose original name was Arouet; leading figure of the 18th century Enlightenment movement (rationalist, liberal, humanitarian, scientific trend of thought of the 18th century); two imprisonments in the Bastile (1717, 1726) and a trip to England (1726–1729) taught him hatred of arbitrary absolutism and admiration of English liberalism; his stormy relationship with Frederick II of Prussia saw him banished from Berlin (1753) but later forgiven; having won a large fortune through gambling, he bought himself a large estate near Geneva (Switzerland) (1758); visited Paris (1778) but was overwhelmed by the triumphal reception he received there and died; the scope of his written works is immense (52 volumes in 1883) plus extensive correspondence; plays include *Zaire* (1732) and *Mérope* (1743); prose tales, notably *Zadig* (1747) and *Candide* (1759) were vehicles for social and political satire; his philosophical works (1734) and (1756) influenced European thought for generations; also wrote historically; he has been regarded as one of the world's great men partly because of his personality; considered an outstanding wit, he was the leading propagandist for 18th century free thought: dignity and equality of all men (despite his own aristocratic ancestry) and freedom of conscience; in his own political and social views, he inclined towards conservatism, but his writings have been seen by some as having ignited the French Revolution (which would have horrified him); *See:* **Common-Sense, Doctor, God, Mistakes, Moderation (× 2)**

WASHINGTON, Brooker T. (1856–1915) American (USA) educator, administrator author; considered the foremost black educator of the 19th and 20th centuries; born a mulatto slave (his mother black, his father an unknown white man) on a Virginia plantation, moved with his mother after emancipation (1862) and the end of the American Civil War (1865) to work packing salt in West Virginia at age 9; a year later became a coal miner (1866–1868) before becoming a house boy for the owner of the mines, whose wife encouraged his education; at age 16 was accepted to Hampton Institute (founded by General Samuel Armstrong, an anti-slavery advocate, to train black teachers); his tuition paid for by a wealthy white sponsor; later taught an experimental school; tried studying law and theology but ended up returning to teaching; one of the founders and leading builder of Tuskegee Institute (1881) in Tuskegee, Alabama, an all-black school; as there was minimal state support ($2,000 a year for the whole school), he went on speaking tours and solicited donations himself; by 1886, the school owned 540 acres, had built their own buildings and had 400 students; by 1900, Tuskegee was the best supported black educational institution in the country (supported by the Rockefeller and Carnegie Foundations); he wrote a widely-read biography *Up From Slavery* (1901); founded the National Negro Business League (1900); became advisor to President Theodore Roosevelt (1901–1909) and President William H. Taft (1909–1913); was the first black person in history to dine with the President at the White House (1901); known as "The Great Accommodater" because of his conservative views that black people should push to attain equality through self-education and improvement of their own economic skills and qualities of character before pushing for the right to vote (a view widely held by northern wealthy whites at the time), in later years he clashed with more aggressive activists (founders of the National Association for the Advancement of Colored People, NAACP, 1909), but, although suffering from arteriosclerosis, he remained a powerful advocate and influence for black people and is honored as the greatest black educator in American (USA) history; *See:* **Success**

WEBSTER, Dave, Ph.D. (Contemporary) American (USA) author; graduate of University of Chicago; founder of The Webster Consulting Group, a health industry management consulting firm; previously an executive with Aventis, one of the world's largest pharmaceutical companies and the Agency for Health Care Policy and Research; *See:* **Time**

WELLAND, Brenda *See:* **Exercise, Power**

WELLINGTON, Arthur Wellesley (1st Duke of Wellesley) (1769–1852) English (United Kingdom of Great Britain) soldier, politician and statesman, Prime Minister (1828–1830); first distinguished himself in the Indian Army (1797–1805); commanded the British Army in the Peninsular War (1808–1814) and at the Battle of Waterloo (1815) at which Napoleon was defeated, gaining the nickname of "The Iron Duke"; attended Congress of Vienna (1815); as Prime Minister repealed the Test and Corporation Acts, passed the (Roman) Catholic Emancipation Act but was unpopular for his opposition to parliamentary reform. *See:* **Sleep**

WESLEY, John (1703–1791) English clergyman, evangelist, poet, writer of hymns (Christian, Protestant originally Anglican, founder of Methodism); at Oxford, led a group with his brother. Charles Wesley (1707–1788 also originally a priest of the Anglican church) who was derisively called Methodists for their painstaking study and religious duties; in London, he experienced a religious conviction of salvation through faith in Christ alone (1738); repudiated Calvinism (1740); said to have preached 40,000 sermons and ridden 250,000 miles mostly on horseback throughout Britain, preaching in the open air, founding Methodist Societies, legally established Methodist societies (1784); inaugurated lay preachers and ordained Dr. Thomas Cooke (1760) for evangelism in America; wrote over 4,500 hymns, among them *Hark, the Herald Angels Sing* and *Jesus, Lover of My Soul;*. *See:* **Life**

WEST, Mae (Ms) (1893–1980) American (USA) entertainer, vaudevillian, comedian, actress (plays and movies), playwright, writer/author, producer; born in Brooklyn, New York, she was a child comedy star in vaudeville by the age of 6; as she grew older, she began writing and performing in plays of her own, was known for her very open, liberal and forward views on sex; her plays were considered scandalous and a threat to public morality; she perfected a persona of a sultry, nonchalant sensuality, with subtle delivery of sexually-charged (often quoted) dialogue; her early plays, *SEX* (1925), *The Pleasure Man* (1928), *Diamond Lil* (1928) and *Constant Sinner* (1931) ultimately got her arrested for indecent behaviour; her first starring movie role (1932) in *She Done Him Wrong* based on her own earlier play, *Diamond Lil* was considered one of her best performances; she wrote her autobiography, *Goodness Had Nothing To Do With It* (1959) and was still performing, at age 85 in a film *Sextette* (1978) but was by then some suffering memory problems and physical ailments that left her acting performance comparatively constrained and awkward; she died 2 years later of natural causes. *See:* **Diary, Personality**

WHORTON, Edith *See:* **Personality**

WHITMAN, WALT (1819–1892) American (USA) poet, philosopher, writer, country school teacher, compositor and editor; started as a teacher, then moved to publishing as a compositor, then a journalist for several newspapers and edited several Brooklyn newspapers (1846–1849); his *Leaves of Grass* (1855 and several subsequent editions) a collection of his free form verse showed him a mystic, a pantheist and a lover of all humanity; he had been an unofficial nurse during the Civil War (1861–1865) and many of his works reflected this; he worked for the government until partially paralyzed (1873), thereafter lived on his writing and lectures in Camden, New Jersey (from 1884); his style of verse has little rhyme or meter, but much oratorical rhythms inspired especially by Old Testament writings; his subject matter celebrated nationalism and the democracy, multiplicity and breadth of opportunity in American society, love, death, the beauty and significance of the human body, and warm human feelings; called "the good gray poet," he was one of America's greatest poets and profoundly influenced poetic form and content, particularly outside America. *See:* **Philosophy**

WILDE, Oscar (Fingall O'Flahertie Wills) (1856–1900) Irish writer, playwright and wit; born Dublin, most remembered works are his witty highly melodic drawing-room nonsense comedies, *Lady Windermere's Fan* (1892) and *The Importance of Being Earnest* (1895); also wrote in a no-nonsense aesthetic novel, *The Picture of Dorian Gray* (1891); and a long poem, *The Ballad of Reading Gaol* (1898) out of his experience in being jailed on morals charges (1895–1897); *De Profundis* (1905) was his apology; *See:* **Criticism, Life, Mystery**

WILLIS, N.P. (Nathanial Parker Willis) (1806–1867) American (USA) poet, author; journalist; political commentator; grew up from age 6 in Boston, graduated from Yale (1827); proud descendant on both sides of his family from early Americans in the New England area who arrived first from England (George Willis, Freeman of Massachusetts, 1638) on his father's side and the Rev. John Bailey (who was preaching in Boston by 1683 after several imprisonments at home in England and Ireland for his non-conformist preachings); his own grandfather had been an apprentice in the same printing office as Benjamin Franklin and was one of the Boston Tea Party (1773) who illegally boarded and threw overboard a large cargo of tea from an East India Company ship in protest of the then Tea Tax being levied from England, and later became the Ohio State printer and a newspaper publisher; his father was a publisher, and he also became a writer, journalist and ultimately a publisher; traveled to England several times; spent his lifetime writing for producing newspapers, journals and poetry; which includes: *The Poems, Sacred, Passionate and Humorous*; *See:* **Jokes**

WILSON, Woodrow (Thomas Woodrow Wilson) (1856–1924) American (USA), orator, politician, university administrator, 27th President of the United States of America (1913–1921); first non-clerical President of Princeton University (1902–1910); Governor of New Jersey (1911–1913); as President of USA (Democrat), his administration lowered tariffs; established the Federal Reserve System (1913); created the Federal Trade Commission (1914); and secured passage of the Clayton Anti-Trust Act (1914); general disorder during the Mexican Revolution had him send U.S. troops to Mexico (1915), to Haiti (1915), to Dominican Republic (1916) and Cuba (1917); during his first term, he fought to keep the U.S. neutral in the European (World War I, 1914–1918) but German submarine warfare brought about the U.S. declaration of war in 1917; he helped establish the terms of peace with Germany, under his proposed Fourteen Points, and attended the Paris Peace Conference (1919); the Treaty of Versailles helped establish the League of Nations (forerunner of the United Nations) but was not ratified by the U.S. Congress; during a speaking tour in September 1919, suffered a breakdown and detached himself from active politics for the remainder of his term; his speeches are considered among the finest of American orators; *See:* **Love**

WINTLE, Walter D., Author from the poem. *"The Man Who Thinks He Can"*; *See:* **Winners**

YANG-MING, Wang (1472–1529) Chinese philosopher; Confucianist, who developed an idealist interpretation of Confucianism that denied the rationalist dualism of the orthodox philosophy; he believed that universal moral law in innate in man and discoverable through self-cultivation; stressed self-awareness and the unity of knowledge and action; said "Intuitive knowledge of good is characteristic of all men; study and self-control should follow the lead of intuitive knowledge"; *See also* **CONFUCIUS** *in this list. See:* **Mistakes**

YEATS, William Butler (1865–1939) Irish poet, playwright and dramatist, ardent Irish nationalist; born Dublin, considered by some to be the greatest 20th century poet to write in English; awarded the Nobel prize in Literature in 1923; leading supporter and wrote for the Abbey Theatre, Dublin; personally attracted by the occult and concerned with Rosicrucianism and theosophy as well as old Irish legend and Irish patriotism; even in his early poems, such as *The Wind Among the Reeds* (1899) were conventionally constructed but notable in their inclusion of Irish mythology and their sense of belonging to the culture of Ireland, themes which continued throughout all his work; some poems elaborated on spiritualism, classical lore, astrology and Eastern philosophy; some were very direct, yet musical, with the simplicity of folk poetry and ardent nationalism; the verse plays he wrote were for the Abbey Theatre; *See:* **Love**

YOUNG, Edward (1683–1765) English poet and dramatist, known best for *The Complaint; or Night Thoughts on Life, Death and Immortality* (1742–1744); a somber blank-verse poem preoccupied with the theme of death. *See:* **Beliefs**

YOUNG, Margaret (1892–1969) (Margaret Young Stafford) American (USA) school teacher, author; Christian (Evangelical Brethren Church); born on a farm near Pauline, Kansas, eldest daughter of a large family, assisted mother in raising siblings as mother frequently ill during her childhood; taught school (1911–15) (at a monthly salary of from $55 to $70 per month); married 1916 (to Jack Stafford), and when her husband accepted a job to manage a copper mine in Chili, she finished her school year and then followed her husband on a solo journey by steamer down the east coast of the United States, through the Panama Canal, then down the west coast of South America to Valparaiso, Chili; lived (and taught school) in the Andes Mountains in Chili in Rancagua for 13 years where her two children were born; returned to the U.S. (1929) but her husband died of pneumonia in South American before he could return (her children were 7 and 9 years of age at that time); began teaching Spanish, bridge and substitute teaching; later became an office manager/bookkeeper of a social agency and worked until the age of 70. *See:* **Life**

Index

About the Author...

DR. ALVIN PETTLE graduated from the University of Toronto Medical School in 1969 and received his fellowship in Obstetrics and Gynecology in 1974. For 20 years he practised at the Etobicoke General Hospital where he delivered close to 10,000 babies in Toronto.

In the fall of 1994, his wife Carol and he opened up a women's wellness centre called the Ruth Pettle Wellness Centre in memory of his mother who died from breast cancer.

Over the last ten years he has co-authored the book *Natural Remedies and Supplements*. He has also produced three audio CD's *The Natural Approach to P.M.S. and Menopause, When Bad Things Happen to Good People,* and *The Scientific Basis of Bio-Identical Hormones*. His video lectures include *12 Steps to Preventing Breast Cancer*.

He continues his life work with Carol in Toronto, surrounded by their five children and six grandchildren.

To order: 1. Mail this form and cheque to Loracal Publishing
2. Visit www.drpettle.com for further details.

Please send me _____ copies of *My Prescription for Life* at $25.00 CDN each, plus $5.00 shipping and handling (Canadian residents please add $3.75 GST and PST). I have enclosed a cheque made payable to Loracal Publishing in the amount of $ _____

Name: _____

Address: _____

_____

City: _____ Province/State: _____

Postal Code/Zip: _____ Phone: _____

Visa/Mastercard: _____ Expiry date: _____
please circle

Mail to: Loracal Publishing
3910 Bathurst Street, Suite 207
Toronto, ON   M3H 5Z3
www.drpettle.com

Please allow 2–4 weeks for delivery